Tax Deductions

and

Efficient Strategies That You Don't Know

Learn Tips And Loopholes To Make Money And Increase Savings

Rishi Buttan

Table of Contents

Introduction

If you are like most people, you have been paying taxes since you began working and just accepted it as part of life. However, since you downloaded this book, you are probably no longer willing to take it as part of life and have become curious about exactly why we pay taxes and what happens to allt the money we deliver to our government. This book has been designed to answer all your tax-related questions. From where taxes originated, how the tax rates have changed and who pays taxes to how corporate taxes work, and what the federal and state governments do with all that money, this book is going to cover it all. This book will also include why some people pay more taxes than others and decide who should pay how much. This book is also going to cover different things you can do throughout the year to help minimize the amount of taxes you are going to pay and contribute to ensuring that you are getting a refund from the IRS after you file your taxes instead of being required to pay the difference because your automatic deductions were too small. Finally, this book will look at the (not very popular) Taxpayer's Bill of Rights and how they benefit you. The tax laws in the United States are complicated and change depending on your situation. However, I hope that when you have finished reading this book, all your questions about the United States taxation system will be answered, including problems that you didn't know you had. After reading this book, you should feel more confident heading into a new tax year.

What Are Taxes

The word tax is defined as being a compulsory contribution to state and federal revenue that the government levies. It is applied to a worker's income, business profits and added to the cost of some goods and services and onto some transactions. If you look at any pay stub or receipt in your house, you will see a spot where you were charged taxes. In the United States, we use something that is called a progressive tax system. This means that higher-income individuals and corporations are taxed at a higher rate than lower-income individual earners. While this means that making less money can keep more of their money, it also complicates the matter of taxes when trying to establish who is responsible for paying what. Later in this book, we will look at how tax rates change based on how much you make and how the more you drive, the more you will pay your taxes.

Where Did Taxes Come From

The history of taxes in the United States is, surprisingly, pretty impressive. The first income tax suggested was during the War of 1812. The idea was based on the concept of taxes that applied to the British Tax Act of 1798. The British Tax Act essentially stated that a progressive tax rate was applied to everyone's income, and the United States developed a similar proposal in 1814. However, since Ghent's treaty was signed in 1815, effectively ending hostilities and the need for additional revenue, the tax wasn't imposed and was forgotten about for a while. In 1861, Congress implemented its first personal income tax to help pay for its war effort in the American Civil War.

The Revenue Act of 1861 stated that all incomes of over USD 800 were required to pay 3%. In 1862 this tax was repealed and replaced with another tax. The Wilson-Gorman Tariff was passed in 1894 by Congress. This was the first-ever peacetime tax. It was a tax of 2% on any income over $4000, which meant that less than 10% of households would be paying taxes. The purpose was to make up for the revenue that was being lost due to tariff reductions. To comply with the act, the New York-based Farmer's Loan & Trust Company announced to its clients that it would pay the tax as well as provide the names for whom the company was acting for, to the collector of internal revenue in the Department of the Treasury, which made them liable for being taxed under the Act.

Among these people was Charles Pollock, a Massachusetts citizen who owned just ten stock shares in the Farmer's Loan & Trust Company. He sued the company to prevent the company from paying the tax. On April 8, 1895, a decision was handed down. It was ruled that the taxes imposed on income from the property by the Wilson-Gorman Act was unconstitutional. The court treated tax on Income from the property to be a direct tax. The Constitution stated that such direct taxes were required to be imposed in proportion to the state's population. Since the tax in question had not been apportioned, it was invalid. After this decision had been reached, the Sixteenth Amendment was proposed and stated that Congress would have the power to collect taxes on any income, regardless of source, and also without regard to census records or any other factors. From that point, taxes continued to be placed and slowly evolved into being what they are today.

About The IRS

The IRS or Internal Revenue Services has been around since 1862 when President Lincoln and Congress enacted an income tax to pay war expenses. At the time, they were called the Bureau of Internal Revenue. The name was changed to the Internal Revenue Service in the 1950s when the agency was reorganized from an investment structure to hired professional employees. The IRS Commissioner and the IRS's chief counsel are selected by the president and confirmed by the Senate. The IRS was reorganized and modernized in 1998 to resemble a model based on the private sector's needs.

Essentially the purpose of the IRS is threefold. First, they are expected to collect the appropriate tax revenue with the least amount of cost. Second, they are expected to serve the public through the improvement of services and products continually. Finally, the IRS is to act in a way that ensures the public remains confident in the department's ability to be fair and efficient while maintaining integrity at all levels.

Income Tax Rates Throughout History

The rates charged for taxes have varied throughout history; the top quality has gone from as low as 7% in 1913 to 94% in 1944 and 1945. Here is a brief look at how the ratios have varied from 1913 until 2012.

- The top tax rate in 1913 was 7% on incomes that were above $500,000. This amount is equivalent to $12 million today.

- At the time of World War One, the top rate rose to 77% on incomes over 1 million dollars. This would be equal to $18.5 million today.

- Top tax rates were reduced in 1921, 1924, 1926, and 1928. In 1928 the top speed was scaled back to 24% for all incomes over $100,000. That is equivalent to $1.38 million today.

- During the Great Depression and World War Two, the income tax rate rose. In 1939, the top speed was 75% and applied to all incomes above $500,000, or $85.1 million. In 1944 and 1945, the maximum speed hit an all-time high at 94%, applied to all payments over $200,000 or $2.69 million today.

During the tax years 1952 and 1953, individuals' marginal tax rate was at 92%.

- From 1964 until 2013, the top income tax threshold has been between $200,000 and $400,000. The one exception was between 1981 and 1986 when the maximum marginal rate was lowered to just 50% for Income above $86,000. From 1988 until 1990, the threshold for paying the top speed was lower, with all incomes over $29,750 paying the maximum rate of 28%.

- In 1992 and 1994, the highest individual tax rates were increased, resulting in a tax increase for all income levels at a rate of 39.6%.

- In 2004, the top individual income taxes were lowered to 35%. And in 2009, the highest-earning 1% of people were required to pay 36.7%.

- In 2012, the two top tax rates were increased to 39.6% and 36%, respectively.

This covers only personal taxes. As well as personal taxes, some taxes need to be paid on properties and for businesses. Now that we understand where taxes came from and what they are, we will look at who pays taxes and why.

Personal Income Taxes

Everyone in the United States pays federal income taxes to the Internal Revenue Services, or IRS, a United States Treasury branch. Many states also have an additional state income tax, and those who don't will be charging many other types of taxes. A tax year is counted as a calendar year, from January 1 to December 31. You are required to have your federal income tax returns filed by April 15. There is an option to file for an extension which will allow you until August 15 to file your taxes. However, this option does not give you an extension on paying your tax liability, so if you choose to go this route, you will have to pay interest on any due taxes.

Tax Withholding

You aren't going to be required to pay all of the taxes on your Income at one time, thanks to something known as tax withholding. When you are working for someone else, your employer is required to make deductions from your pay. Two of these deductions are federal income tax and state income tax, if applicable. Your employer is also going to deduct social security and Medicare contributions. You will know how much your employer has deducted from your pay to put towards your income taxes because they will be required to give you a Form W-2, a wage and tax statement, by January 31.

If you are working for yourself, you will have to make quarterly payments of your estimated taxes to the federal and state governments. If you neglect to do this, you will have to pay a large penalty and interest in addition to the taxes you owe.

Progressive Income Tax

In the United States, the Income that you pay is called a progressive tax. This means that those who make more money are required to pay more in taxes than those who make less. Someone who makes very little money will be required to pay little to no taxes, while someone who makes hundreds of thousands of dollars each year will be required to pay more. The tax system was designed this way based on the theory that those who have more money aren't worried about feeding their families and can contribute more to their government.

Tax Brackets

When it comes to figuring out who will have to pay what amounts in taxes, the IRS uses tax brackets. A tax bracket is a variety of incomes that are taxed at a specific rate. The tax bracket you fall into will be determined by how much you make and how you are filing. There are five different filing statuses you can use when you file your taxes.

Single Filing Status – This pertains to you if you were not married or legally separated on the last day of the year and don't fall into another filing status category.

Married Filing Jointly Filing Status – This is applicable when your spouse and yourself agree to file a joint return – your total combined income and deductions are reported.

Married Filing Separately Filing Status – If you and your spouse don't agree to file jointly, you are responsible for your tax. Occasionally, this method of filing will result in fewer taxes than filing a joint return.

Head Of Household Filing Status – To qualify for this status, on the last day of the year, you must be (a) unmarried or considered unmarried, (b) you have paid more than half the cost of living for the year, and (c) you have had an eligible person living with you for more than half the year (excluding temporary absences).

Qualifying Widow(er) With Dependent Children Filing Status – That status applies to those who lost a spouse in the last tax year to allow them to file a joint return still.

Here is an example of how tax brackets are determined based on the 2015 tax brackets.

Single Filers:

10% - Up to $9,225

15% - $9,226 to $37,450

25% - $37,451 to $90,750

28% - $90,751 to $189,300

33% - $189,301 to $411,500

35% - $411,501 to $413,200

39.6% - $413,201 or more

Married, filing jointly or qualifying widow(er)s:

10% - Up to $18,450

15% - $18,451 to $74,900

25% - $74,901 to $151,200

28% - $151,201 to $230,450

33% - $230,451 to $411,500

35% - $411,501 to $464,850

39.6% - $464,851 or more

Married Filing Separately:

10% - Up to $9,225

15% - $9,226 to $37,450

25% - $37,451 to $75,600

28% - $75,601 to $115,225

33% - $115,226 to $205,750

35% - $205,751 to $232,425

39.6% - $262,426 or more

Head Of Household:

10% - Up to $13,150

15% - $13,151 to $50,200

25% - $50,201 to $129,600

28% - $129,601 to $209,850

33% - $209,851 to $411,500

35% - $411,501 to $439,000

39.6% - $439,001 or more

To better explain how this works, we will look at two people who both file their taxes in the single bracket and how much tax they will be required to pay. Keep in mind, this isn't considering any potential deductions, but just their Income and how it would be taxed. This will give you a better idea of how those who make more money end up being taxed much higher than those who make less.

Person One: This person makes a total of $31,998 for the year.

On the first $9,225: 9,225 * 10% = $922.50

On the balance of $9,225 to $31,998: $31,998 - $9,225 = $22,773 then $22,773 * 15% = $3,415.95

Which makes their taxes a total of: $922.50 + $3,415.95 = $2,493.45 or 7.79% of their total income.

Person 2: This person makes $248,685 for the year. This person makes a total of $31,998 for the year.

On the first $9,225: 9,225 * 10% = $922.50

On the balance of $9,225 to $37,450: $37,450 - $9,225 = $28,224 then $28,224 * 15% = $4,233.60

On the balance of $37,451 to $90,750: $90,750 - $37,451= $53,299 then $53,299 * 25% = $13,324.75

On the balance of $90,751 to $189,300: $189,300 - $90,751= $98,549 then $98,549 * 28% = $27,593.72

On the balance of $189,301 to $248,685: $248,685 - $189,301= $59,384 then $59,384 * 33% = $19,596.72

Which makes their taxes a total of: $922.50 + $4,233.60 + $13,324.75 + $27,593.72 + $19,596.72 = $65,661.29 or 26.4% of their total income.

As you can see, those who make more money will end up paying a significantly higher percentage of their overall Income towards their federal income tax. However, this was without any deductions being claimed. When you consider hypotheses, these numbers are going to change. However, a person who makes a higher income will pay a higher percentage of their income towards taxes, even if it isn't as drastic as the example above makes it seem.

The Capital Gain Loophole

All money you make during the year is counted as income, regardless of where it comes from, and that can throw things off. For example, if you are working at a job for a wage, that is Income. If you win the lottery or even find a twenty-dollar bill on the street, those are income. There is one exception to this rule. If you buy and sell stocks or pieces of companies and profit, capital gains and not payment. This is how the very wealthy make a lot of their money by investing. Investing in stocks is a glorified way of gambling when you look at the bare bones of it. You are purchasing pieces of a company in the hopes that the company will do well and you will be able to sell the stocks and make money. If you take one thousand dollars and go to the casino and successfully gamble it and win one hundred thousand dollars, you are going to have to pay income tax on ninety-nine thousand dollars. Now, if you take the same one thousand dollars and buy stocks with it, and then sell the stocks for one hundred thousand dollars, the money you have made from the stores is not Income, but instead capital gain, which means that you are only going to end up paying about half the amount of income tax on it.

This isn't the only place where the wealthy is awarded tax breaks. If you are working for a wage and decide that you will buy yourself something with your money, you will have to pay a sales tax on that purchase. This is true whether it's a can of beer, a car, or a new TV. The tax will vary based on what you are buying and where you are buying it, but you are being charged tax. However, when the wealthy use their money to buy and sell pieces of companies, they aren't required to pay a tax on the purchase price.

While these points may make it seem as though the wealthier you are, the fewer taxes you pay, you have to remember that the more personal Income you have in a year, the higher your tax rate is. Think about the example we did above. While the wealthy can soften this a little bit, overall, they are still contributing more to the government tax pool than someone who makes less money. Companies are also taxed. However, the tax system for a company is different from individual taxes. We will look more in-depth at how companies pay their taxes, but first, we will look at some of the other personal taxes that a person will settle outside of their income taxes.

Chapter 1

Following Tax Guidelines

Now that you have a clear idea of what tax accounting is and how it's different from financial accounting, you need to be familiar with basic tax guidelines. After all, tax accounting's primary goal is to ensure proper compliance with tax regulations, i.e., filing the right kinds and amounts of taxes and doing so on time. Here are the most important things you must know about tax accounting for your business as a business owner.

Hobby or Business

Are you into hobbies that also double as extra income sources like baking, video editing, or songwriting? While all income sources are subject to tax return requirements, there are different rules for reporting Income from hobbies and businesses. If a side business involves a favorite hobby, consider these tips for taking advantage of special regulations and limits for tax deductions on the Income.

Tip #1: Determine If It's a Business or Hobby

One of the key characteristics of businesses is that they're profit-oriented (obviously). In contrast, you engage in hobbies and interests for the sheer pleasure of it. Income, if any, is just a by-product.

To help you objectively determine whether what you're doing is a business or a hobby for taxation purposes, the IRS recommends considering the following factors:

➤ Whether you carry on the activity in a businesslike manner and maintain complete and accurate books and records

➤ Whether the time and effort you put into the activity indicate you intend to make it profitable

➤ Whether you depend on income from the activity for your livelihood

➤ Whether your losses are due to circumstances beyond your control or are expected in the startup phase for your business type

➤ Whether you change your methods of operation in an attempt to improve profitability

➤ Whether you or your advisors have the knowledge needed to carry on the activity as a successful business

➤ Whether you succeeded in making a profit in similar activities in the past

➤ Whether the activity makes a profit in a few years and how much profit it makes

➤ Whether you can expect to make a future profit from the appreciation of the assets used in the activity

Tip #2: Know the Allowed Hobby-Related Deductions

As a taxpayer, you can – within specific limits – deduct ordinary and necessary expenses related to your hobbies for tax return purposes. Everyday expenses are those that are par for the activity, i.e., accepted and expected. Essential costs are those that apply to the hobby.

Let's say you're a handyman and making furniture is one of your hobbies. Examples of ordinary and necessary expenses are raw materials such as wood, nails, and paint.

Tip #3: Learn the Limits on Hobby-Related Deductions

To maximize tax deductions from hobby-related activities, you must know the limits. The maximum amount of tax deductions you can enjoy from hobbies is the Income associated with such activities. Unlike business losses, i.e., when operating expenses exceed revenues or Income, losses from hobbies cannot be used as tax deductions for other Income.

Tip #4: Know How to Deduct Expenses Related to Your Hobby

More than just knowing what and how much to deduct, you must also know how to do it properly. In general, you'll need to itemize all hobby-related deductions on your tax return, which may fall into one of three kinds of beliefs, each having special rules. IRS Publication 535 provides clear instructions on how to do it.

Record Keeping Guidelines

Ensuring good record keeping for tax and financial accounting purposes has a countless number of benefits. These include:

- ➢ The ability to monitor your business's progress or digress accurately
- ➢ Accurate financial statements
- ➢ Clear identification of income sources
- ➢ Keeping track of tax-deductible expenses
- ➢ Accurate and timely payment and filing of tax returns

Given the many kinds of documents and financial records, your business uses and creates in its operations, which of them should you keep? While the IRS doesn't require particular types of forms for businesses, the kind of business you own will determine the types of documents that require marking. But in general, these include bank statements, official receipts issued and obtained, and invoices, among others. For tax accounting purposes, all financial documents evidencing Income and expenses need to be retained.

For how long should you keep records? Ideally, for long. It's because you'll never know when you'll need to show proof for specific transactions and claims, but if resource constraints prevent you from keeping all documents from day one, consider the IRS' prescriptions (from their website) for how long you should keep records for income tax purposes:

- ✓ Three years if situations (4), (5), and (6) below do not apply to you
- ✓ Three years from when the original return was filed, or two years from when the tax was paid, whichever comes last, if you file a claim for credit or refund after you file your return

- ✓ Seven years if you file a claim about losses arising from writing off bad-debts or worthless financial securities
- ✓ Six years if you do not report the Income you were supposed to, and it's above 25% of the gross income reported on the return
- ✓ Indefinitely if you do not file a return
- ✓ Indefinitely if you file a fraudulent return
- ✓ Keep employment tax records for at least four years after the date that the tax becomes due or is paid, whichever is later

For your employees' withholding taxes, you must keep records for the last four years at the minimum.

When you file your or your business's tax returns, you're responsible for proving the authenticity of all information in them, such as entries, deductions, and statements. Often called the burden of proof if your business practices excellent record-keeping, substantiating information in your tax returns will not be problematic or stressful.

Buy a Vehicle

A person can deduct expenses on buying a car for their business and that they can buy an Electric vehicle and use tax credits to pay little to nothing on the car on tax deductions if they have a business. As mentioned earlier, you can use the mileage deduction strategy to reduce your taxable income. Many small business owners use this method to reduce the taxes they pay. If your business uses a large SUV or truck, you should consider buying a vehicle that will be more than 6000 pounds. As mentioned earlier, the current deduction is $1,000,000, but this depends on your business usage and the cost of the vehicle. Since that is an increase in the deduction, it will vary drastically among a truck, RV, and SUV. Always discuss these options with your advisor.

The Tax Year

When filing tax returns, you need to determine your taxable Income within the taxable or tax year. This refers to the annual accounting period for record-keeping and income/expense reporting to the IRS. Remember that a yearly accounting period excludes short tax years.

You have two options for determining your business's tax year. These are calendar and fiscal. When you choose a calendar tax year or calendar year, your business's annual accounting period begins every 1st of January and culminates at the end of December 31. If you choose a fiscal year, the tax year is 12 consecutive months ending on the final day of the 12th month, except for December. It can be from February 1 to January 31 of the following year or June 1 to May 31 of the next year.

By default, your business adopts a tax year when you fill out its first income tax return based on that tax year, but a specific tax year is sometimes required, in which case, it's the default one. A required tax year is one that the IRS and tax regulations require.

Many taxpayers mistakenly think they have specifically adopted a tax year while they haven't. Don't make the same mistake. Doing the following doesn't mean you have adopted a tax year for your business:

- ✓ Applying to extend the deadline for income tax return filing
- ✓ Submitting an employer identification number (EIN)
- ✓ Paying estimated taxes for the current tax year.

Once you file your business's initial tax return using a calendar year, there are only two ways to change to a fiscal year. The first is with express IRS approval, and the second is if your enterprise meets specific exceptions found in Form 1128, i.e., Application to Adopt, Change, or Retain a Tax Year.

Usually, any business can adopt either a calendar or a fiscal tax year. The calendar year is your only option if:

- ✓ Your business neither keeps records nor maintains accounting books
- ✓ It has no annual accounting period
- ✓ The business's current tax year doesn't qualify as fiscal
- ✓ Income tax regulations of the Internal Revenue Code mandates your business explicitly to use a calendar year
- ✓ Short Tax Years
- ✓ This refers to those that are less than 12 months, which the IRS may require when your business – as a taxable entity – has:
- ✓ Existed for less than a full tax year
- ✓ Changed its accounting period

In the first scenario where your business hasn't existed for 12 consecutive months yet, it still needs to file a tax return for the number of months it had earned Income. Fortunately, the tax-filing requirements and tax determination process are the same as for full ones, i.e., 12 months, that end on the last day of short tax years. If you want more information on this, check out IRS Publication 538 on Accounting Periods and Methods.

If you decide to change your business's accounting period at a later time, you will need approval from the IRS to do so, using its Form 1128, i.e., Application to Adopt, Change, or Retain a Tax Year. Unless your application qualifies for automatic approval, an IRS ruling in favor of the tax year change and payment of a user fee is required.

Tax Audits

As a small business owner, you'll be very hands-on in managing your enterprise. You may be consumed with high-level functions like:

a) Acquiring new clients or expanding market share

b) Business innovations

c) Customer service

d) Hiring staff

e) Strategizing

f) Making money

Not only are record-keeping and tax accounting tedious and time-consuming, but they also don't contribute to the bottom-line. Hence, the chances are that you will put much less consideration for these. This can put you at risk during tax audits because of possible tax computing mistakes. Many entrepreneurs, tiny business owners consider tax audits terrible news. It also doesn't help that audits, regardless of conducted by the IRS or an external auditor, can disrupt normal operations.

Now that you're aware of these make avoiding tax audits one of your business's top priorities. While it can't avoid getting audited, understanding the most common IRS red flags for tax audits and avoiding them can help your business minimize the chances of catching the IRS attention. Here are those red flags that you should avoid as much as possible:

Multiple and Consecutive Net Annual Losses

If your business reported net losses for three out of the last five tax years, the IRS would likely give it a friendly visit. Those chances are even higher if yours is a sole proprietorship because of the tendency to co-mingle personal and business funds. Hence, prepare for a tax audit if these happen. One of the best ways to minimize the risk of incurring at least three years of net losses in five years is to review your business' revenues and deductions, making sure they're accurate and reasonable. You may need to forego deductions if only to avoid red flagging your business to the IRS with more than two unprofitable years out of five.

Habitually Late Filing of Returns

Submitting your business' tax returns past the deadline isn't just costly. It also draws the IRS' attention and increases the likelihood of a tax audit. So, ensuring the timely filing of tax returns doesn't just save you money but also minimizes tax audit risks. This is one area where procrastination shouldn't be tolerated, not even a whiff.

Excessive Salaries

If your business offers shares of the company to employees, you'll need to be cautious about giving them reasonable salaries. Why? Put, company shareholders also earning large wages from the company draw the IRS like flowers attract bees. This will not likely be the most severe issue your business may face if tax is audited. The chances are that the more significant concern would be if the enterprise continues to rake in more money with each passing year. To minimize this risk, make sure you have a good grasp of the average salary for employees in your industry. That way, you can structure salaries competitively but not excessively. This can help you avoid being on the IRS' tax audit radar.

Countless Number of Deductions

While deductions are essential for minimizing your business's taxes, you need to use them wisely. Not every expense qualifies as legitimate deductions for business purposes. If you have the habit of charging just about every cost under the sun as deductions, you increase the likelihood of drawing the IRS's attention. This is especially true if you're operating a sole proprietorship. Worse, once the IRS discovers your business's excessive and unqualified deductions, it may impose penalties.

To avoid getting flagged for too many deductions, review your business's premises for the last few years for consistency. But if you just started a new business, better to check with an accountant to ensure you only charge ordinary and necessary expenses as deductions for your business per IRS guidance.

Large Donations to Charities

While giving such can be a very noble endeavor, it's better to err on the side of caution by keeping the amounts moderate or low. Why? Giving vast sums of money to charity often provides the IRS with the impression that a business is up to something. It's because many companies use charitable donations as a way to avoid taxes. The IRS considers this as a blatant abuse of the internal revenue code, which can severely punish. Make it a win-win situation for your business and its benefactors by giving reasonable donations consistently every year, regardless of how high or low its earnings are. This provides the practice with a semblance of normalcy, which is crucial for avoiding the IRS' radar and, consequently, tax audits.

Excessive Use of the Business' Vehicle

Especially for a sole proprietorship, claiming full business use of your vehicle puts the business at high risk for catching the eye of tax authorities and inviting them to conduct a tax audit. When deducting a vehicle's business use for tax purposes, you have the option of using the actual amount of expense, the IRS standard mileage rate, or both throughout a tax year, but using them both when filing tax returns is a glaring red flag for the IRS. Claiming 100% business use for depreciating a vehicle also requires documentary evidence for every trip the car was used for.

To minimize your business's risks for being red-flagged by the IRS for excessive business use of vehicles, it's crucial that you carefully consider how they're used and ensure only the essential business-related services are claimed for tax-filing purposes. Only the following may be good business-related uses of vehicles:

- ✓ Going to client meetings
- ✓ Traveling to conduct research
- ✓ Posting mail for the business

✓ Any other activities directly related to your business

Using the car to go for a gym workout or drive your spouse to work isn't justifiable business-related vehicle uses.

Transacting in Cash

Believe it or not, but if your business deals mostly in cash, its chances of catching the eye of tax authorities are much higher. Why? It's because verifying Income earned in money can be way harder compared to non-cash transactions. Also, large purchases (equipment, vehicles, properties, etc.) using cash isn't par for the course and usually cause concern. Why not pay in check or via credit card, both of which are far safer and more practical than lugging around a ton of cash? Those who do so usually try to hide something, and what they're trying to hide is illegal.

To avoid getting red-flagged because of this, use a cheque, credit, or debit card for high-ticket purchases. But if you're more comfortable using cash or if transactions require it, just ensure high-precision and details in recording them and establish clear paper trails through documents like official receipts, invoices, etc. And for single buyer receipts for amounts greater than $10,000 within 12 months, make sure to fill out Form 8300 completely.

Rounded Numbers and Erroneous Calculations

One of the most common problems small business owners face when they do their tax returns results from using numbers rounded instead of exact figures. This practice often results in erroneous tax return calculations, a red flag for the IRS to do a tax audit. To minimize your business's risks for flagging due to wrongly calculated tax figures, avoid using averages or rounding off numbers to the nearest dollar. Instead, always use decimal points when calculating earnings and expenses for tax return filing purposes.

Use Schedule C Filings Carefully

As a sole proprietor, you will need to use schedule C form 1040 to calculate your business's tax deductions. These may include expenses such as interest paid on loans, advertising, and Home Office deductions. Why should you be very careful when using this form? Many experts think this increases the likelihood of being audited by the IRS. But this doesn't mean you should avoid it altogether. It shouldn't have to be a choice between getting tax audited or weaving your rights to tax deductions, especially those that are legitimate and valid. Just be very careful about the assumptions you will claim, both in kind and amount, to avoid catching tax authorities' unwanted attention.

If it's your first time getting into the business or not yet familiar with tax accounting, it's best to seek professional advice. That is why I can never overemphasize the benefit of letting a professional tax accountant do the work for your business.

Not Reporting Taxable Income

If ever there's such a thing as a mortal sin to the Internal Revenue Service, that would be a failure to report all of your business's taxable income. Especially for small business owners like you, tax authorities expect to report all income earned within the United States, including Income kept in offshore accounts, payments received in cash, and other kinds of Income. You can be sure that the IRS will come knock-ing at your business's door to conduct a tax audit if they see you fail to report all of your business's taxable income.

As a small business owner, especially if you're a sole proprietor, you need to maintain well-organized and kept records and avoid commin-gling personal and business assets and liabilities. Doing so ensures you avoid non-reporting of taxable Income, even if unintentional. Remem-ber, the IRS doesn't distinguish between erroneous and intentional un-derreporting of taxable income. They will still penalize infractions the same way.

Claiming Losses on Rentals

Under certain conditions, claiming losses from rentals in real estate businesses are allowed, but doing this isn't as easy or straightforward as it sounds. For one, claiming such failures is the same as wearing a bright neon shirt while running in the dark. It makes your business even more visible to the tax authorities and increases its chances of being subjected to a tax audit. If you want to take advantage of actual rental losses by claiming them in your business's tax returns, let a sea-soned tax accountant do it. Doing so minimizes the chances of errone-ous computations, and if ever your business is audited, it will not be considered a finding.

Excluding Foreign-Earned Income

This would only apply to you if you are a small business owner that either works out of the country for a significant portion of a tax year, you make money overseas, or both. If this is you, you can be eligible to claim exclusions on the Income you earn abroad, but having stringent and rigid requirements for claiming these will most likely catch the IRS's attention and subject you to a tax audit. So, consult with a tax accountant who has experience with such exclusions to minimize your risks.

Using Cryptocurrencies

Because cryptocurrencies such as Ethereum and Bitcoin are relatively new financial assets and are considered autonomous from any Regulatory agency, using them in your business can make the IRS interested and conduct an audit. Being beyond regulating governments, these are often used for funding criminal activities. The best thing you can do with cryptocurrencies is to limit them to your personal use. That way, you won't tick off tax authorities.

During Tax Audits

As soon as the IRS notifies you of an impending tax audit, contact your accountant right away. If you don't have one by the time a tax audit is due, I highly recommend hiring a tax accountant as soon as possible. Preferably, he or she must be on board by the time tax authorities conduct the audit.

- There are other things you can do to get through tax audits with minimal stress and complications. These include:
- Keep a positive attitude. This is even more important during your interactions with IRS agents. To make the entire audit process move smoothly and quickly, always be courteous and honest when dealing with them.

- Make sure your financial records are well organized. By doing this, it will be easy for you to present supporting documents for the transactions IRS agents may look into. When your records are in disarray, submitting valuable forms may become difficult and give agents the impression that something is up, even when things are every day.

- Always be transparent and honest. With your accountant, always strive to present all required documents so you can clearly and honestly support your income tax computations to the auditors.

- Read all IRS notices. Ignoring them will neither prevent an audit from happening nor get you through one once it starts.

As a small business owner, preparing taxes is already challenging. Can you imagine the added stress of being audited by the IRS, too? If your business gets tax audited, be ready for a comprehensive and sometimes extended process. It's because tax authorities will probably ask you lots of questions and ask for many documents to show your reported Income and deductions' accuracy and legitimacy.

Being aware of the misconceptions regarding tax audits can also help you prepare for them well. Some of these include:

- Low-income taxpayers don't get audited. Small businesses and sole proprietors can also be subject to tax audits regardless of how big or small their incomes are.

- The time frame covered by tax audits is limited to just one year. If you think this is the case, you're in big trouble. The Internal Revenue Service has up to three years to audit the tax returns you filed for your business. So, don't be complacent, thinking you will no longer be audited just because the tax season is over.

- Your business's tax returns can be audit-proofed. Yes, the red flag tips presented above can help minimize the chances of your business being tax audited, but that does not mean you are guaranteed to escape tax audits. All taxpayers are eligible to be tax audited, and the best thing that can happen is to minimize the chances of winning this tax lottery.

Chapter 2

The Easiest Way To Immediately Reduce your Taxes

Congratulations! You are the proud owner of one of America's greatest treasures: The Small Business. Without question, our country is truly the "Land of Opportunity." And Small Business Owners like you are the main reason why.

Congratulations on taking the first step to "going it alone." There are probably as many reasons for starting a Small Business as people who have created a Small Business. Undoubtedly, the most common reason for starting a Small Business is the most obvious one: to make money.

Running a Small Business successfully (and by that, I mean profitably) is a tremendous challenge. There is a multitude of obstacles to making money in your business. And perhaps the most frustrating one that stands in the way of your success is taxes.

We live in a great country, for sure. But our "system" is not without its problems. And one of the most significant issues you face as a Small Business Owners is simply this: "How can I legally reduce my tax bill?"

Taxes: Income Tax, Payroll Tax, Sales Tax, Real Estate Tax, Personal Property Tax, Excise Tax. The seemingly never-ending list of tariffs is just that -- a never-ending list. It does not end.

And not only is our tax system "never-ending but" it is also incredibly frustrating because of its complexity.

Just how complicated is The Tax Code? Consider this: Way back in 1913, when federal income taxes first began, the entire Tax Code occupied a mere half-inch thick book. The first federal income tax return was a simple two-page form with four pages of instructions.

Now what do we have? -- A literal monster! Today the Tax Code takes two four-inch-thick volumes to print, along with well over a million lines of "regulations" that officially explain and interpret what the Code means. When you add all the relevant tax-related Court decisions that apply the Code -- well, now we're talking about 25 feet of library shelves.

With all these tax regulations, what's the average taxpayer to do? I realize just how intimidating the Tax Code can be to a Small Business owner like yourself. That's why I wrote this book -- to help people like you discover the best ways to lower your tax bill legally.

The first legal loophole is this: Given the same amount of profit, not all businesses pay the same amount of taxes.

Think about that for a moment. It's probably something that you've always wondered about; maybe we're even a bit "suspicious" about. Well, if you ever thought that some people pay less tax than you (even though they make the same amount of Income), you are correct.

Why is that?

Is it fair?

Is it right?

Is it legal?

Yes, it is legal for one business owner to pay less tax than another business owner, even though both have the same Income.

Why does this happen? I will answer this question by explaining the easiest (and perhaps the most overlooked) tax-reduction strategy on the books. Many small business owners are paying too much tax because they own the wrong type of business.

Now, what do I mean by the wrong type of business?

I'm not talking about type in the sense of whether you own a Carpet Cleaning Business vs. a Pet Store. I don't mean what industry your business is in. I don't mean whether you are a manufacturer, a wholesaler, a retailer, or a service business.

Very only, I'm talking about whether your business is a Sole Proprietorship, a Partnership, a "C" corporation, an "S" Corporation, or a Limited Liability Company.

There are several types of business ownership from a legal entity standpoint. And you have got to get this right, or you will pay thousands of dollars more in taxes than you should.

I certainly don't want to waste your time going into all the legal pros and cons of how your business should be structured legally. But the simple fact is, there are significant differences in the amount of taxes that each of these business entities usually pays.

And there are probably some very compelling reasons you picked the type of business structure you currently have. Maybe you have received legal counsel on this matter, and your attorney has told you the best way to go from a legal standpoint.

I'd like you to consider the possibility that if your business is a Sole Proprietorship, you could be paying more tax than necessary simply because you are a Sole Proprietorship. And if you would give serious consideration to incorporating your business and choosing to have it taxed as an S Corporation, you could save thousands of dollars in taxes for many years to come.

Tax-Saving Tip #2 – Making the Switch

If your business is a Sole Proprietorship, please read this next section carefully. This is probably the most important information about taxes you will ever read.

IMPORTANT: No matter what type of business you own, please read this section. If you are a Partner in a Partnership, or a member/owner of an LLC, or even a corporation shareholder, do not skip this section. You must understand the concepts explained here, no matter what type of business you own. In other words, this section is not just for Sole Proprietors. You'll see what I'm talking about after reading this section and the sections that follow.

Sole Proprietors pay more tax than "S" Corporations because of something known as Self-Employment Tax. As a Sole Proprietor, you report your business profit on your Income Tax Return via Schedule C (Profit or Loss From Business). Your business profit is added to any other income reported on your tax return (form W-2 wages, interest, and dividends, or whatever) and is then subject to regular income tax.

But the Sole Proprietor not only pays income tax on his/her business profit. The business profit is also subject to Self-Employment Tax, which is also reported on the Sole Proprietor's tax return via Schedule SE (Self-Employment Tax).

This Self-Employment Tax is the equivalent of the Social Security Tax and Medicare Tax (also known as Payroll Taxes) that employees and employers pay on wages. The combined total of Social Security Tax on wages is 12.4% (the employee pays 6.2% and the employer pays 6.2%). The combined total of Medicare Tax on wages is 2.9% (the employee pays 1.45%, and the employer pays 1.45%). Altogether, then, a total of 15.3% of employee wages is paid to the government for Payroll Taxes (Social Security and Medicare taxes).

So, if you are an employee, you pay half, and your employer pays half. I'm not here to debate whether an employee ever really gets his/her money's worth out of that 7.65%, but at least the employee only has to pay half of the 15.3%.

The Sole Proprietor, on the other hand, has to pay the full 15.3%.

For purposes of the Self-Employment Tax, the Sole Proprietor is, in effect, treated as both the employer and the employee. I'm sorry to give you the bad news, but that's just the way the system works.

(To be technically correct, the way Schedule SE works, the Sole Proprietor does get a tiny break on the 15.3% Self-Employment Tax. For purposes of this discussion -- let's say that the Sole Proprietor ends up paying about 15% Self-Employment Tax on his/her business profit.)

So let's look at an example of a Sole Proprietor's Self-Employment Tax. Let's assume that your business profit, as reported on Schedule C, is $50,000.

Schedule C Profit $50,000

Self-Employment Tax Rate x 15%

Self-Employment Tax $7,500

Now, let's assume that this same business is an "S" Corporation rather than a Sole Proprietorship.

The business has the same $50,000 profit reported on the corporation's income tax return (Form the 1120S).

Here's how the "S" Corporation owner ends up paying less tax than the Sole Proprietor.

Let's also assume that the "S" Corporation is run very similarly to the Sole Proprietorship. It's a typical one-person show. The owner does most, if not all, of the work.

So, since the business is a Corporation, not a Sole Proprietorship, the company must pay the owner as an employee. In other words, at least some of the $50,000 profit must be paid to the Owner/Employee as wages.

Let's assume that the Fair Market Value of the Owner/Employee's services rendered to the business is about $35,000. In other words, if the "S" Corporation owner went out and hired someone else to do the work, the "S" Corp would have to pay someone $35,000 in wages to do the same job that the owner usually does.

Now here's where the tax savings come in . . . .

Only the $35,000 in Owner/Shareholder wages would be subject to the 15.3% Payroll Tax.

Of the $50,000 "S" Corporation business profit, only $35,000 is subject to Payroll Taxes. The other $15,000 in profit legally avoids Payroll Tax. If the business is run as a Sole Proprietorship, the entire $50,000 is subject to Self-Employment Tax (Payroll Taxes).

TAKE A LOOK:

"S" Corporation Wages $35,000

Payroll Tax Rate x 15%

Payroll Tax $5,250

Now, let's compare the two scenarios:

SOLE PROPRIETOR: Self-Employment Tax --$7,500

"S" CORPORATION: Payroll Tax --$5,250

TAX SAVINGS FOR THE "S" CORPORATION --$2,250

By only running your business as an "S" Corporation rather than a Sole Proprietorship, you can save $2,250 in taxes. And assuming that you have this kind of profit year after year, you would save $11,250 over five years and $22,500 over ten years.

PLEASE NOTE that these tax savings is NOT a saving in income tax. It is a saving in Payroll Tax (paid by the corporation) vs. Self-Employment Tax (produced by the Sole Proprietorship).

All other things being equal, there are no savings in income tax in the above scenario. Assuming $50,000 of business profit, the Sole Proprietor and the "S" Corporation Owner/Employee would pay the same amount of income tax (again, assuming all other things equal).

So, if you are currently running your business as a Sole Proprietorship, some substantial tax savings are waiting for you by merely forming an "S" Corporation.

Chapter 3

Income Tax

On the federal, state, and even local levels, taxes are imposed on individuals based on their Income. The tax systems that are prevalent within the jurisdiction of the state would define what taxable Income is. Many states tend to refer to the federal concepts while they are determining the taxable income.

A brief history of income tax in the US

While you are probably sorting through all the receipts, or perhaps when you are studying the latest amendments made to the US laws of income tax, you might have wondered about how this ritual had even come into being in the first place. You might have wondered about this tradition that goes up to the 15th of April. To provide you some clarity about these questions, let us briefly look at the history of income tax in the US. The 16th amendment passed by Congress on the 2nd of July in the year 1909 was ratified in 1913 on February 3rd, and this contains the origins of how tax levied on individuals have come into being. But the historical evidence predates the amendment ratified by Congress.

The Revenue Act of 1861 passed during the Civil War by Congress had provisions relating to personal income tax to pay for the war expenses. These taxes were, however, repealed after ten years. However, in the year 1894, Congress had enacted a Federal income tax at a fixed rate, and this was ruled out as being unconstitutional by the Supreme Court of the U.S. because it was a direct tax and it should be apportioned depending upon the population of each state, and a fixed rate isn't ideal. The 16th amendment that was later ratified in 1913 had done away with the objection mentioned above. This allowed the Federal government to tax individuals' Income without paying any heed to the state's population.

In the 1950s, the taxation system was further reorganized, which replaced the patronage system with career employees. The IRS Restructuring and Reform Act that was passed in the year 1998 had been the starting point for reorganization as well as modernization of the IRS on a wide scale after almost half a century of its establishment, and it also prompted for the establishment of the Taxpayer Advocate Service as an independent wing inside the agency for the taxpayer. April 15th is the deadline for the filing of taxes, but it wasn't so initially. The date specified by the Congress in 1913 was March 1st after the 16th amendment was passed. In the year 1918, Congress had decided to push this date a little ahead to the 15th of March, and it remained so until the tax overhaul that took place in the year 1954, and this date was once again shifted on to the 15th of April. And this is how the date for the filing of the deadline has come into being.

About Federal income tax

Perhaps the most debated, complicated, and visible tax that is levied is the federal income tax in the U.S. The national income ratification of the 16th amendment to the USA constitution took place in 1913, which established the federal income tax. The federal income tax is levied on wages and salaries and all the Income you might have made from different sources. It includes the receipts of interest, dividends, capital gains, if any, the Income from self-employment, alimony, and prizes. For understanding the basic concept of federal income tax, you need to understand just two significant issues. The first issue is that not all the income you receive is taxable. There is a lot of difference between total revenue, adjusted gross income, and taxable income. The second issue you need to understand is the difference between the effective tax rate and the marginal tax rate. So, let us get a better understanding of all these concepts.

Total Income is the sum of all the Income that an individual or a couple receives from different sources. Generally, for most people, the central portion of their total revenue comes from their wages or salaries. Many also receive Income from their various investments, and this Income tends to come in the form of interest, dividends, and capital gains. The Income from self-employment will also be included in an individual's total income; income received in alimony, farm income, and even the

Income from gambling. The amount of federal taxes that a person owes is not calculated based on their total revenue.

Once the tax filers have obtained their total Income, they can subtract some expenses from their total Income since they are non-taxable. We arrive at adjustable gross Income, referred to as AGI, after the non-taxable costs have been deducted from the total revenue. These expenses could include the contributions made to an individual's retirement account, any moving expenses, interest on student loans, tuition fees, and other costs. AGI is important because most of the IRS's tax data is sorted on this basis. However, before you jump to any conclusions, the income tax is not calculated on this Income. Taxable Income is the amount you arrive at once you have subtracted the deductions and various exemptions.

Deductions can be either itemized or standard. The standard deduction would be an amount that is fixed and is excluded from taxation altogether. This rate keeps changing every year. Tax filers also have the availability of an option to itemize all their deductions. To enumerate your beliefs as a taxpayer, you will need to add up certain expenses incurred during the year. These expenses would include state taxes, taxes on real estate, interest on mortgages, gifts made to charities, and any other significant medical fees. If the itemized deductions happen to be a more considerable sum than standard deductions, then the itemized deductions will be subtracted. Exemptions are usually calculated based on the number of dependents and the number of tax filers altogether. For instance, a single tax filer with no dependent children can claim up to one exemption, whereas a married couple with no children can claim up to two exemptions. Each dependent child is counted as a single exemption, and additional exemptions are also provided for those above 65 years of age or blind.

Taxable Income is arrived at by subtracting the deductions as the provided exemptions from the AGI. This happens to be the amount that a taxpayer tends actually to pay taxes for. However, you need to understand that this amount is not just multiple taxable incomes, and it isn't based on a single tax rate. The federal system of taxation in the US is based on the increasing marginal rates; this means that different tax rates are to be applied to other portions of an individual's income. Not all income is taxed to the same quality of marginal taxes. Income from capital gains on investments is taxed at a lower rate than the income from labor.

According to the taxation system in the U.S., individuals, corporations, trusts, and even estates are subject to the levy of income tax. Whereas partnerships aren't taxed, their partners are subject to income tax on their respective shares of Income and all the applicable deductions and can take their credit claims. Some types of business entities also have the option of being treated as partnerships or even corporations. Taxpayers are required to file for their tax returns and also to self-assess their taxes. Taxes can be paid by withholding a certain amount from the monthly paychecks. In case the taxes aren't covered by the withholdings, then the excess amount needs to be made in the form of quarterly payments. The tax returns filed are subject to review and also adjustment by the government authorities. As mentioned earlier, certain deductions are permitted to make; these could be business and even non-business expenses. Most of the state and the federal tax system in the U.S. levy taxes on the income of its citizens and residents worldwide. For foreign income taxes, a federal foreign tax credit is granted by the government. Residents who are living abroad can also claim the exclusion of foreign earned income. Individuals needn't be residents of a specific state but can be residents or even citizens of the United States. Many states also tend to grant a credit similar to this for taxes paid to other states. These credits are usually limited to only the amount of tax levied on income from foreign sources.

Graduated tax rates

The income tax rates levied on a federal and state level differ for various corporations and individuals. When the rate of Income is higher, then even the taxes are higher. Depending upon the filing status, the rates of taxation for individuals also tend to differ. The percentage of Income at which the rate of taxation starts tends to be higher for a married couple that is filing returns jointly or for a single individual filing as the head of the household; this means that the tax rate is low. The quality of taxation that applies to individuals varies from 10% to 39.6%; the tax levied on corporations differs from 15% to 35%. The state income tax rates also vary from 1% to about 16%, including the local taxes whenever they are applicable. While computing the federal income tax, you can deduct the state and local taxes you might have paid.

Business entities

Corporations are liable to pay tax on their taxable income that is separate from that of their shareholders. Shareholders are also subject to tax that they need to spend on the dividends they receive from the corporations. The same rules don't bind partnerships. But then again, its partners should calculate their taxes by including the various items from the league. The corporations that U.S. citizens or residents wholly own can elect to be treated as a partnership instead of a corporation. Charitable institutions are also subject to tax on the business income that they make. Certain transactions contracted by these entities aren't subject to taxation, including formation or even reorganization. There are various tax credits available that can reduce income tax at both the federal and state levels. Some credits are available only to individuals in particular. This includes a child tax credit for every dependent child, the credit for the education expenses borne, and those for the low-wage earners.

Payment or withholding of taxes

The system of taxation that exists at both the federal and state levels is self-assessment. Taxpayers are bound to declare and also pay tax without assessment by any of the tax authorities. The extent of taxes that haven't been paid through withholding needs to be paid in quarterly payments. Employers are responsible for withholding from wages the income tax, social security, and also Medicare taxes. The amounts that are to be withheld by the employers need to be based upon the employees' representations in the W-4 form that the employees fill out.

State variations

They levied taxes by different states, and localities vary and can be fixed or even graduated taxes. Forty-three states and many of the localities in the U.S. have decided to impose income tax on individuals, whereas 47 states and many localities have decided to impose tariffs on Income generated by corporations. Most of the rates tend to be similar for all types of payments. State and local income taxes are levied in addition to the federal income tax, and these taxes can be shown as deductions while calculating the federal income tax. The state law determines these taxes, and it is generally based on the notional taxable Income. The state rules for taxation tend to vary regarding the individual itemized deductions. Most states don't allow for any determination from the state income taxes levied on individuals and corporations. They can also decide to levy taxes on specific incomes that are exempt at a federal level. States that are imposing income tax on the payments of individuals and corporations tax all of them and Income earned by others who might not be the residents of such a state but earned the concerned state's revenue. Businesses imposed an income tax in a state only when they tend to have sufficient connection to that state.

Reporting and payment

According to how the jurisdiction provides, employers are duty-bound to report all the payroll taxes to the appropriate taxing authorities. In most jurisdictions, they need to submit the quarterly reporting that includes the aggregate of the income tax withholding and the social security taxes required to be paid. Employers must file such aggregate reports of the unemployment tax on a quarterly or an annual basis according to the state's laws at a state and federal level, respectively. Every employer is supposed to provide the employee with a yearly report on the W2 form of the IRS on the wages paid and the taxes being withheld at the federal, state, and local levels. This form signifies the payment of tax on behalf of the employee. They are required to pay the payroll taxes to any of the taxation authorities depending upon the rules. Payment of many federal and state-level payroll taxes needs to be made by transferring electronic funds when it crosses a certain threshold.

Penalties

There are specific penalties for the nonpayment or the timely payment of taxes. If not paid, the federal payroll taxes will have a sentence ranging from 2% to 10%. There are similar states as well as local disadvantages that are applicable as well. When you fail to pay your proper monthly or quarterly payments, then you are subjected to further additional penalties. An automatic penalty of $50 is imposed whenever you don't file the W-2 Forms correctly or in a timely fashion. The state and local penalties levied will depend upon the respective jurisdictions. There are particularly severe penalties that can be imposed when the social security and the federal income taxes aren't paid to the IRS as per the dues. A sentence that can go up to 100% of the total amount paid can be levied upon the employer or any other person or entity who had complete control or custody of such funds from which these payments were to be made.

Chapter 4

What has to be reported as Income?

Let us first be clear of which incomes are taxable. Two categories of payments can be subject to taxes: revenues you earned and payments you don't make. Earned incomes encompass salaries, wages, tips, bonuses, sick pay, unemployment benefits, commissions, and certain noncash fringe benefits.

Unearned incomes include interest, profit from the sale of estates, dividends, rents, royalties, winnings from games of chance, alimony, and business and farm incomes.

In some situations, you can be exempted from tax payments. An individual's taxation depends on their gross income, so when defining your Income, you have to report all taxable income, including taxable scholarships. Non-taxable scholarships do not be listed since they are not liable to taxation and serve educational purposes. Your scholarship is taxable when in the form of a paycheck in exchange for tutoring, research teaching, and other services you might enjoy under the scholarship. It is referred to as study-work income.

Fringe Benefits

Fringe benefits include services and other perks which the employer pays for an employee, e.g., transportation. Fringe benefits are usually taxable unless stated otherwise by law. A cafeteria plan represents a list of your employer's services that you would like to receive instead of cash. A cafeteria plan includes accident benefits and health benefits (but, be careful, since the Archer medical savings accounts (Archer MSAs) or long-term care insurance is not part of the deal), adoption assistance, dependent care assistance, health savings accounts, group term life insurance payments (along with costs that cannot be excluded from salaries).

Benefits that cannot qualify as cafeteria plan benefits are Archer medical savings accounts, minimal services, athletic facilities, educational assistance, employee discounts, cell phones from employer, meals, reimbursements for moving costs, retirement plan, transport, tuition reduction, working condition benefits, scholarships, and fellowships.

W2 is the form all the fringe benefits will be included on as taxable. The perks provided by the employer can vary from beautiful gifts, like rent or cars, to smaller ones. The benefits' value will be calculated according to their fair market value and costs on the market. The IRS also provides guidelines for estimating the weight. Employers could be subject to high penalty fees if they fail to report all the benefits provided adequately for their employees.

Capital Gains & Losses

Capital gains refer to profits a person earns when selling a capital asset, such as property, stocks, shares, bonds, or mutual fund shares. According to tax law, we have long-term and short-term capital profits. Short-term capital gains are defined as profits that you earn from selling an asset that has been in your ownership no longer than a year. Short-term capital gains can be very tricky when it comes to taxation. The highest tax rate is applied to this kind of sale, where you will have to pay a 43.3% rate. This might discourage you from selling newly acquired assets and wait until they reach long-term status.

Long-term capital gains are profits coming from sold assets that have been in your ownership for more than a year. They are significantly lower, with tax rates starting from 0%, 15%, or 20% for the last year.

We already mentioned the short-term gains maximum tax rate, which could be even liable to an additional surtax for Medicare up to almost 37%, but that depends on your Income.

When it comes to taxed long-term gains, low taxpayers (bracket 10/15%) can even hope for a 0% rate, while other taxpayers will have to pay the 15% or 20% tax rate unless otherwise exempted from it under tax law. Always look at exemptions in the tax law because you may be in a tax-exempt category.

Real estate capital gains in depreciation come with a 25% tax rate unless you are a low taxpayer (10 and 15% bracket).

Capital losses are defined as capital asset sale losses (e.g., stock, real estate, bond, mutual fund). Losses are also broken into short-term and long-term capital losses. Capital losses can generate deductions, and they are to be reported to tax authorities only if expected to rise in value. They can be said to secure deductions on the tax return.

We also have realized & unrealized losses, as well as recognizable gains. Unrealized losses are not reported and refer to losses where the asset you bought drops in value, but you do not sell it immediately. Instead, wait until its value increases again, and then sell it. You can only report when the actual sale happened, referred to as realized loss (assuming that you still sold it under the price you purchased it at).

Capital gains and losses are now filed on a new form introduced not so long ago by the IRS. The 8949 form facilitates the process, offering a comparison between gains and losses provided by investment companies. Capital losses allow you to get back at least some of your losses via tax returns, which is still something.

Traditional IRA (Internal Revenue Service) and Roth IRA

Many US citizens do not know which retirement account to use...so which one is better? The traditional IRA account or the Roth IRA account? Let us explain the difference between them to decide which one would be right for you. An individual retirement account can impact not only you but also your family in defining your long-term savings. The traditional IRA is suitable for all persons who earned incomes and are under the age of 70, whereas the Roth IRA comes with specific criteria that have to be met by an individual.

To contribute to a Roth IRA, your incomes have to be below a specified amount defined by the IRS. The amount can vary from year to year. The amount that makes you eligible also depends on your marital status and how you earned that Income. Usually, your payments should be achieved (e.g., work), resulting from non-earning revenues such as rentals and investment. How the IRS specifies the amounts and limits depends on the modified adjusted gross income. Be aware that the numbers, i.e., specified amounts, can change. Single households and heads of households must have an annual income lower than $116,000 to qualify for Roth, while in 2016, the amount was specified at less than $132,000, and we can only wait to see what it is going to be in 2017.

A married couple who filed jointly must have had an income lower than $183,000 in 2015 and less than $194,000 in 2016.

Separate filing of married couples was an option if their annual income was less than $10,000.

So, if you fall under any of the given categories, you can file for a Roth IRA contribution, but further on, the savings limits for retirement also depend on your age. Married and single persons under 50 can contribute $5,500 to their IRA Roth fund. In the case of a married couple, where one spouse is employed and the other is not, it is still possible to set aside $5,500 for each.

For persons over 50, the same amount contribution applies, only with the addition that they can set aside another $1,000, which makes up for a $6,500 limit on total Roth contribution for persons from age 50 onwards.

Rental Income

Rental income, as already mentioned, is also subject to taxes. Renters should record their rental expenses and landlords, including cost, revenue, and costs. To keep it neat and organized, landlords may use spreadsheets or software for finances which are mass-used these days. As a landlord, you should list property management commissions, cleaning, maintenance, repair expenses, advertisement expenses, real estate taxes, mortgage interest rate costs, security deposits, utility costs, trash, etc. Bear in mind to list the price at which the apartment or house was bought and the real estate's annual depreciation.

Losses from a rental property can also be used to squeeze out certain deductions since passive activity losses are deductible.

Rents do not always generate net profit since the rent fee usually covers the mortgage, repairs, property tax, and sometimes insurance. Once the property depreciation is added, it can turn out that the landlord's expenses are higher than profits from renting. If the loss is $25,000 or more, the landlord can count on the passive activity limitations set at this exact amount, which means that the landlord cannot lose more than $25,000 within a tax year.

If you are a landlord and want to sell your property that you have rented so far, you need to know that it differs from selling your private house or apartment in which you live in. It involves subtracting the cost basis from the selling price.

What life insurance Deductions can be claimed?

The Medical Reimbursement Plan (MRP) described below works best for "C" Corporations and Sole Proprietorships. "S" Corporations and

Partnerships can also have a MRP, but the tax benefits are not as great. One of the most misunderstood aspects of tax law concerns the deductibility of medical expenses. Many people may have a vague idea that medical expenses are deductible on their personal income tax returns, but over the years I have become acutely aware that most people are just plain clueless about this. Yes, medical expenses are potentially deductible on your personal income tax return, provided you meet both of the following two conditions:

1. You itemize deductions on Schedule A.

So if you take the standard deduction, forget about deducting any medical expenses. And remember, it is only advantageous to itemize deductions if your total itemized deductions exceed your standard deduction.

2. Your medical deductions exceed 10% of your Adjusted Gross Income (AGI)

Adjusted Gross Income is simply your gross income less any adjustments like a deductible IRA contribution. As an example, let's say your AGI is $50,000. Multiply $50,000 times 10% to get the magic number of $5,000. You can deduct medical expenses only to the extent that your medical expenses exceed $5,000. In other words, your first $5,000 of medical expenses is not deductible. If you have $6,000 of medical expenses, the first $5,000 ($50,000 x 10%) is non-deductible; only $1,000 is deductible.

So you can see how tough it is to deduct medical expenses on your personal income tax return. The large majority of taxpayers are not eligible to take this deduction, and now that you understand how the rule works, it is easy to understand why.

Of course, many people are covered by an employer-sponsored health insurance plan, and often these plans provide excellent coverage at affordable group rates. So employees of large companies may not have to worry too much about medical expenses. There may be a deductible and co-insurance payments, so out-of-pocket medical costs may only be a few hundred dollars per year. And if a more major medical problem occurs, like a serious illness or accident, often a very high percentage (say 80% or 90%) of the employee's medical cost is covered.

But what about the small business owner like yourself. Now that you have formed your own business, you may not have an employer-sponsored health insurance plan to rely on. Small business owners frequently must purchase health insurance on their own, and often must pay much higher insurance premiums than a large company gets on a group plan. And an individually purchased plan may not provide the same level of benefits -- resulting in higher deductibles, higher co-payments, and more out-of-pocket expenditures.

Well, there is a way for the small business owner to save taxes by deducting 100% of his/her medical expenses, including health insurance premiums. This strategy is known as a Medical Reimbursement Plan (MRP). The MRP utilizes IRS Code Section 105, which allows small business owners to deduct 100% of their insurance premiums and out-of-pocket medical expenses not covered by insurance.

Let's use the above example: You have $6,000 of medical expenses. Assuming you have $50,000 of AGI and are able itemize deductions on your personal income tax return, only $1,000 of these medical expenses are deductible. If you are in the 15% federal income tax bracket, this will reduce your taxes by only $150 ($1,000 x 15%).

Instead, your business establishes a Section 105 Medical Reimbursement Plan. Let's also assume that you are the business' only employee. So now you simply submit documentation of your medical expenses to your business (which is you), and the business reimburses you the $6,000. Now the full $6,000 of medical expenses is fully deductible by the business as a legitimate business expense. Assuming the business is in the 15% tax bracket, this results in an income tax savings of $900 rather than $150.

To make this arrangement even better, there are payroll tax savings as well. These reimbursed medical expenses (in the above example -- $6,000) are not considered taxable compensation (i.e. wages or salary) to the shareholder/employee. Had this $6,000 been paid to the shareholder/employee as wages/salary, the business and the employee would have paid of total of 15.3% in social security/medicare payroll taxes (7.65% paid by the business plus 7.65% paid the employee). So, $918 in payroll taxes was saved by paying this $6,000 as a tax-free fringe benefit rather than as taxable compensation.

Of course, the higher your medical expenses, the higher your tax savings. And don't forget that the MRP can reimburse you for both health insurance premiums and out-of-pocket medical expenses not covered by insurance.

To create the MRP requires some careful planning and formal paper-work. Here's an overview of what to do.

STEP ONE: Formal adoption of the Medical Reimbursement Plan

The business must formally adopt a Section 105 Medical Reimburse-ment Plan, subject to the non-discrimination rules and regulations es-tablished by the Department of Labor. This means that you must offer the MRP to all employees who meet eligibility requirements, including any non-family employees.

A word of caution is in order here: If you have non-family employees who meet the eligibility requirements, you may not want to establish the MRP. It may be too expensive to pay all eligible employee medical expenses.

The most common situation for effective utilization of the MRP is a "one-person" corporation or a family-owned corporation in which all employees are family members. The most common example is a cor-poration which is 100% owned by one person, and that one person is the only employee of the corporation. Another good example would be a corporation with just a few family-member shareholders, and the only employees are the shareholders and immediate family-members of the shareholders. Then the corporation's liability to reimburse em-ployee medical expenses is limited to the family members who own the corporation.

Another common scenario for the MRP to work well involves a Sole Proprietorship in which one spouse is the Owner of the business and the other spouse is an employee of the business.

This concept of limited exposure is critical because the MRP must comply with the non-discrimination rules and regulations of the Department of Labor. You, the employer, must establish the eligibility requirements that your employees must meet to participate in the plan. The following list of eligibility requirements show the maximum requirement allowed:

1. Hours -- Any employee working at least 25 hours/week must be included in the plan
2. Seasonal Employees -- Any employee that works at least seven months/year must be included in the plan
3. Age -- any employee over age 25 must be included in the plan
4. Current Employees -- Any current employee who has worked for you more than 36 months must be included in the plan
5. New Employee -- Any future employee who completes 36 months of service for you must be included in the plan.

A few comments about the about list of eligibility requirements:

You may select any of these requirements up to the maximum allowed, but you are also permitted to select a lower requirement for participation. For example, if you choose to exclude employees based upon the number of hours worked, you may choose to exclude employees who do not complete 20 hours of work per week, even though the maximum exclusion is 25 hours per week. This would exclude any employee who works less than 20 hours/week, and would include any employee that works at least 20 hours/week.

The ability to select a lower requirement applies to any of the regulations for participation in the MRP.

Any of the regulations listed above may exclude an employee from participating in the MRP.

IMPORTANT: If you choose not to select any eligibility requirements, all employees will be eligible for participation.

So, if you have non-family employees and you want to limit your re-imbursement exposure, study these eligibility requirements closely. It may be possible to still hire non-family employees and legally exclude them from the MRP, provided you follow these MRP setup rules carefully. For example, you could utilize the 25 hour/week requirement to legally exclude all part-time employees. Maybe your business can be run with non-family employees only working part-time (25 hours/week or less). The only full-time employees (more than 25 hours/week) would be family-member employees.

This step of formal adoption of the MRP is critical. Plan documents must be created that meet the above-mentioned non-discrimination rules and regulations established by the Department of Labor. Do not treat this step lightly. If you think that your business is a candidate for a MRP, please consult a tax professional.

STEP TWO: Implementation of the Medical Reimbursement Plan

Here's where common sense and good record-keeping come in to play. If this is a real Medical Reimbursement Plan, then the employee must submit documentation to the business of the employee's medical expenses, and the business must reimburse the employee for those expenses. In other words, the employee must provide receipts for the expenses and the business must then pay the employee for the expenses with a check from the business checking account. It is critical that these simple paperwork procedures be followed. Do not treat the reimbursement procedure casually.

Chapter 5

Reduce Taxable Income

It is difficult and confusing to understand small business taxes. As a small business owner, you may have several questions about how much you have to pay, why you have to spend so much, how you can reduce the taxable income, and when you need to pay. You can also use some tips to reduce the taxable income legitimately and reduce the tax you pay to the government. Unfortunately, most small business owners, especially those who do their taxes on their own, overpay their taxes since they miss out on some deductions. They also find it challenging to manage their business and retirement savings efficiently for tax purposes.

The US tax code is 70,000 pages long, and, understandably, a small business owner and many accountants have trouble navigating through the tax code. It would help if you dealt with many complexities when you try to minimize the tax bill. If you have the right strategies in hand, you can save money on taxes and make your life easier during the tax season. This chapter leaves you with ten tips you can use to reduce the taxable income.

Look at the Adjusted Gross Income

Many limitations, additional taxes, and tax breaks will tee off of the adjusted gross income. You can modify this amount to calculate the adjusted gross income. For example, you can avoid paying the 1% additional Medicare tax on the earned income if the adjusted gross income does not exceed $200,000. The new tax reform does have many tax cuts, but you must pay this amount every year towards Obamacare.

Use an Accountable to Reimburse

If you reimburse employees for tools, entertainment, travel, and other costs, you should do this using a plan to meet the IRS's requirements. This plan is known as the accountable plan. When you have this plan, you can deduct the expenses but not report the reimbursements as income to the employee. This will save the company an additional employment tax and also lower the taxable income.

If the company does not have an accountable plan to reimburse the employees, they will soon ask for one. Under the new tax reform, an employer cannot deduct any miscellaneous unreimbursed employee expenses from their tax filing. When you give your employees an accountable plan for reimbursements, it will help them save money on taxes and help the business.

Use Smart Tax Elections

You can use multiple ways to reduce taxable income. All you must do is be strategic about the business expenditures. For example, you can deduct the cost of acquiring any equipment or machinery full up to a specific dollar amount. In 2018, this amount was increased to $1,000,000. That said, if you are just starting your business and it is not profitable yet, you can ask your accountant to help you depreciate the value for these items in your balance sheets and financial statements. This is a better thing to do for your overall tax situation. You should spread the value of the purchases across future tax years and not deduct the full price at once. This will help you predict any deductions for the coming years where the asset will be more valuable.

For instance, if your taxable income falls under the 15% tax bracket, but now you expect to be in the 35% tax bracket due to increased profitability, a deduction of $10,000 in your current financial statements will only help you save $1500 in taxes. When you depreciate the amount for five or seven years, it will produce a total savings of $3500 in the 35% tax bracket. You can ask your accountant about deducting medical expenses based on their actual costs or using the IRS's mileage allowance. You can also ask them how you can remove the home office expenses. If you choose to use the IRS simplified rate, the current standard deduction will be $5 per square foot of your house.

Another method you can use to save taxes is to claim for disaster losses. You can also consider deducting any business insurance expenses that you pay every year. The IRS form 1040 will help you determine the business insurance deduction you can claim. You can remove the following business insurance coverage in the state.

- Commercial Auto Insurance
- General Liability Insurance

- Business Interruption Insurance
- Workers' Compensation Insurance

Since unscrupulous people develop small businesses to cheat on taxes, the IRS has started to scrutinize the filings made by small businesses. It does this to ensure that the companies are legitimate businesses and not tax shelters. If your business is registered as one of the following, you should consider seeking professional assistance to understand what insurance premiums you can deduct from your tax amount:

- Sole proprietorship
- A single person limited liability company
- Separate entities
- Consider Carryovers

The IRS places some limitations on deductions and credits. These limitations will prevent you from using them fully in the current financial year, but you can carry them over to future years. This is one of the best ways to reduce taxable income. You should keep track of your carryovers, so you do not forget to use them when you file taxes in future years. If you use tax software or a program, it will do this automatically for you. If you hire a tax professional, you can ask them to bear these carryovers in mind. Some of these carryovers include the following:

- General business credits
- Net operating losses (limited to 80% of taxable income)
- Capital losses
- Home office deduction

- Charitable contribution deductions

- Extract Income Using Tax-Free Methods

The distribution of your share of business profits, bonuses, and salaries are taxable. You can benefit from your success without paying any taxes, which means you do not have to pay taxes on all your profits. It would help if you considered talking to your accountant about the following:

- The inclusion of tax-free fringe benefits, including health savings accounts, retirement plans, and medical coverage.

- The loans made by the business to you and any low or no interest investments or loans. If the loan rate is lower than this defined rate, the company will have to report the interest from the arrangement. If the interest rates are meager, it is not too costly to do this.

It is sometimes better to abandon property rather than to sell it. If you have a property that does not add any value to you or the business, you can speak to the accountant to determine and understand the benefits of abandoning it. This will allow the company to take an ordinary loss instead of a capital loss, and you can use this as a deduction. Remember, capital losses are also subject to limitations.

Fringe Employee Benefit Plans

Any additional wages that you pay employees will increase the employment tax that your business should pay. If the company does pay specific fringe benefits for the employees, you can avoid paying taxes on these benefits. The following are some benefits you can offer your employees, and these are tax exempt.

- Transportation benefits
- Disability insurance
- Health insurance sponsored by your business
- Meals provided for employee convenience
- Dependent care assistance
- Group term life insurance
- Educational assistance
- Long-term care insurance

Employ a Family Member

One of the easiest ways for you to reduce taxes is to hire a family member. The IRS allows various options with the benefit of helping you shelter your taxable income from the different tax rates. You will receive a higher rebate if you hire your children. According to a certified public accountant and founder of Sound Accounting, Scott Goble, you can lower the marginal tax rate and eliminate the tax you pay as income to your children when you hire a family member.

For instance, a proprietorship does not have to pay any Medicare taxes or Social Security taxes on a child's wages. They also do not have to pay the Federal unemployment tax. The earnings, however, must come from a justifiable business source. The IRS will allow a small business owner to benefit from hiring a spouse. They can reduce their taxes by doing this. You can also set aside a retirement fund for your family members, depending on the state's benefits.

Move Profit to Retirement Plan

It is effortless to set up a retirement plan for every employee in your business. This is similar to a tax-deferred retirement plan that any corporate or large business offers its employees. You can give employees this option so that they can make contributions to their future. These contributions are tax-deductible. The employee will not have to pay any contribution they make towards these retirement plans. The time in savings funds will grow on a tax-deferred basis, which means any distribution taken in the future is taxable.

Employees can choose from several retirement plan options depending on their situation. Remember, if you have many employees, you must ensure that you cover every employee in your business. You cannot favor the management or the owners. If you choose a plan such as the 401(k), it will shift the employees' cost-savings benefits and give them the flexibility and choice to plan for their future. Most small businesses prefer to give their employees this option to a defined benefit pension plan. If they choose to offer pension plans, the burden will fall on the employer. When you set up a retirement plan for your employees, you will qualify for a tax credit.

Plan for the Year-End

As mentioned earlier, you cannot plan your taxes only at the end of the financial year. You can, however, save a lot of money if you prepare for the financial year at the start of the year. You can use different strategies to help you reduce the taxable income the year ends.

Don't Note the Amount from Suppliers until your Receive Payment

If your business uses the cash accounting method, you can delay billings for any work that you complete at the end of the year until the customer or client pays you for that service. This will help you lower the tax you owe the government in the current year. Remember, never defer income if you have a cash shortfall or have any concerns about the customers' ability to pay you.

Claim Immediate Depreciation on Fixed Assets

You can also lower the taxable income in the current financial year by appreciating the recently purchased asset. It would help if you revalued the assets in your books. This will help you lower the net profits since you increase the depreciation in your accounts. If an investment does not have any value or use, you can ask the accountant to delete it from your books.

Write Off Bad Debt

If a customer still has to pay you money, and if it seems unlikely that he will, then you can write this amount off as a bad debt. This amount is one that you cannot claim or collect. This deduction is known as a bad debt deduction. You can consider this amount as a loss, allowing you to reduce your losses and profits. Having said that, if you must qualify for the deduction, you should include a bad debt in your business income. It would help if you consisted of this transaction as a loan to the client, supplier, etc.

Submit Taxes on Time

While planning your year-end, it is good to have the taxes filed and submitted on time. You can ask for an extension from the IRS, but several penalties will apply for late filing. Remember to pay on time, even if you choose to extend the filing of your taxes.

You can make some changes to your taxes within the first quarter of the next financial year or even if the previous financial year is over. This will help you save some money on your last year's taxes. It is essential to do this when there are many changes made to the tax laws.

Restructure the Business

If you run the business as a sole proprietor or partner with another individual, it is time to choose a new business structure. We have looked at different methods you can use to do this earlier in the book.

You should reduce the amount of taxes you pay by taking advantage of the various opportunities and breaks available. It is up to you to discover any new ways and methods to lower taxes for your business. Remember, this is especially true when you entered 2020. Any moves you make now will help you save a significant amount of money this year and in the years to come.

Chapter 6

Procedures for Identifying Tax Lien Properties

As noted earlier, each state has its own rules and regulations on how to handle tax liens. Even then, the basics are always similar. First, you will need to register early enough if you want to participate in tax lien auctions. Therefore, determine the state, county, or city where you wish to join as an investor, and then register as soon as possible.

As soon as your registration is complete and verified, you will have to research the intended tax lien. There is much more than just the value of a home. There are renovations and other works that go into a home: Potential for rental property, ease of resale, and so much more. This goes to show how crucial proper research is. As such, you need to follow the procedure listed below.

- Carefully read all documents, understand what each document states exactly, and determine whether the information contained therein is accurate and verifiable.

- Determine the current estimated value of the home. You could use the value of other homes in the area to gauge the weight.

- Take the time to drive by a property and take a good look at it. Just a visual look at a property can help you understand what it looks like.

- Only after you perform this due diligence should you then determine whether a property is worth investing in or not.

- When you finally decide that a property is worth investing in, you should then attend the auction and place your bid. Be very careful when placing bids. Most are very competitive, so avoid the trap of overpaying as you will eventually lose out.

- In case you win a bid, you should immediately take charge of the lien as you are now officially the owner of the tax lien.

- In most cases, delinquent homeowners eventually pay their taxes, and you will receive the interest payments due to you. However, if the property owner fails to meet their tax obligations, you will eventually become the property owner.

Tax Lien Certificate Buying Procedures

Count the costs

Purchasing a lien is entirely different from purchasing real property. When you invest in a lien, you essentially sign up to pay all the unpaid property taxes. However, you will be the next in line to purchase the property should it come to that. Even then, it is your responsibility to ensure that the property is in such excellent condition that you can make good returns from it. Also, keep in mind that there are additional costs to the lien, including specific fees and tax payments. These have to be paid upfront.

Verify the lien

You will need to verify the lien on a property before buying. The reason is that some liens contain wrong information, such as the incorrect address, and so on. Also, you need to collect enough data on a property, like the property's value, taxes owed, the owner's name, and so on. You will need this information, especially if the property owner files for bankruptcy or if you perhaps discover that the property is government-owned. Things could head south if you buy a lien, and then additional information surfaces. For instance, if the owner makes part payment of their back taxes or perhaps files for bankruptcy, then the lien will become invalid.

Examine and inspect the property

You should inspect a property before buying a lien. This way, you will determine whether the property is worth investing in and if the amount charged is worth the lien. There are cases where properties lose value because of certain factors such as general neglect, industrial chemicals pollution, and even natural disasters like storms. An on-site inspection is advisable because of zoning laws that determine businesses set up in a particular area.

Read the local laws

Laws govern tax liens and their eventual sales, and each jurisdiction has its laws and regulations. As such, you need to with the local agencies and state authorities to find out what rules and restrictions apply to tax liens locally. Sometimes, laws vary from state to state, so reading and confirming all laws about a particular jurisdiction is useful.

Take the example of the state of New Jersey. Tax lien holders in the state have the right to be compensated first, should the property be foreclosed. In other conditions, such as Arizona, you will be expected to pay all subsequent taxes on a property after buying a lien. If you fail to do so, then the lien will be sold to another investor. This is why it is crucial to read about local laws in each jurisdiction from where you wish to buy liens.

How to Bid on a Tax Lien Property

Buying tax lien certificates is different from all other auctions. While the bidding system varies between jurisdictions, there are certain similarities. Bidding strategies are dependent on specific rules and regulations governing the sale of tax liens. There are those with strict rules, while others have more flexible procedures and processes. Here are a couple of tips that will enable you to place your bids successfully.

1. Use the bid-down approach.

The bid-down method is used when investing in tax liens. Traditionally, bidders bid upwards, meaning they raise the price of the bid. However, in this instance, it is advisable to bid down the interest. This way, bidders determine how low the interest rates get and the levels they will accept when purchasing a tax lien. Remember, though, that your profit margins will depend on the interest rates, so avoid bidding too low. The bottom line as an investor is to put your money in investments that bring in a reasonable return, so bidding too low is a strategy to avoid.

2. Bid down on the ownership.

Another alternative bidding approach that you can consider is bidding down on property ownership. This is not a very advisable approach when purchasing a tax lien certificate. It only occurs in individual states, such as Iowa. In this instance, the property will be valued downwards such that the eventual bid winner will receive a lower income. Remember that your payment and interest will be based on the property's value, so a lower property value means reduced income.

3. Premium Bidding

This approach in tax lien bidding is very similar to traditional bidding. The auction is held, and the eventual winner is the bidder who offers the highest premium over the lien. Premium bidding often happens in situations where a tax lien was already auctioned but found no takers. This underscores the importance of carrying out your due diligence before buying.

4. Random Selection

Some counties and municipalities prefer the random selection approach. According to the authorities in these localities, the belief is that this approach is the best for allowing investors to invest in the tax liens. Under this approach, all bidders are given a number, and the numbers are drawn together. The bidder whose number is called first and accepts the price wins. If the bidder turns down the offer, another number will be removed, and the process repeats in that order.

5. Off-the-Shelf Purchase

Another approach that you are likely to come across is where you get to buy tax liens directly from the tax office within a specific jurisdiction. This often occurs in cases where tax liens were auctioned but found no willing buyers. Again, before investing in such tax liens, take time to do your due diligence. Check out the property and find out if it is worth investing in.

Crucial Points to Know About Tax Lien Bidding

There are a couple of essential facts that you need to know when investing in tax liens. The first is that there is often tough competition for tax liens on properties. The competition does not just come from individual investors but also large investors, money managers, hedge funds, and lien investment funds.

Due to the stiff competition, the rates tend to go down drastically. This can have a drastic effect on an otherwise lucrative investment opportunity. However, apart from interest rates, there are other things to look forward to.

More than just interest rates

While interest rates sometimes fall drastically, you can expect to receive additional income from penalties charged on the amount due. Sometimes, interest rates as high as 18% have been brought down to levels of almost 0% due to intense bidding by investors.

They are hoping to earn penalty fees and get the sole rights should there be a subsequent tax lien on the same property at the initial 18% rate. This is something that happens in states such as New Jersey. Since liens are issued quarterly, bidders tend to forfeit interest on the initial lien just to earn a full 18% on the second and other subsequent liens.

Lien investing requires patience and cash.

In some cases, you will find that you need a lot more capital to invest in tax liens than you thought. The reason is that sometimes additional liens are issued on top of existing liens. In this case, new liens take precedence over old liens. As such, investors will have to buy the new liens to protect their interests in the property.

Apart from cash, you also need patience because tax lien investing can take time. Mostly you will need to wait upwards of 4 months, or at least 120 days. You will need to invest time and money into research and due diligence. You will also have to attend auctions and bidding in person and handle the paperwork. Therefore, if you do not have a lot of time on your hands, you may find it a tricky affair.

Buy tax liens closer to your home.

You should find out a home's value before investing in it. Typically, the tax bill is often 3% or less than the value of the house. However, it could be higher for undeveloped land. Knowing the value of a property is advisable before investing. A property that is closer to home is more comfortable to view. All that you need to do is simply drive by and take a look.

Stock market and investing in real estate.

If a given company's stock qualifies as a "small business stock," then 50% of the revenue generated when selling the stock will be exempted from profit earned, while the other 50% generated from the sales will be taxed. This is usually done at an effective rate of 14%. Under § 1244, a $50,000 deduction ($100,000 if jointly filed in marriage) is available as an ordinary loss if the company fails.

C Corporations – Drawbacks

C Corporations, as faultless as it may appear, have some significant drawbacks as well. The truth is that there is no business structure without a fault; what matters is the ability to fit in what works for you as a business owner. The following are some drawbacks of a C corporation.

Double Tax: I bet no business owner likes tax; it becomes more disheartening when you are double taxed.

Here is a quick fact - Most C Corporation owners pay tax accruing to their business and also personal income tax. Well, that's what a dividend is: An after-tax allocation of company assets that are also paid on your return. Consequently, the business' profits can also become double-taxed once the company is transferred or dissolved.

Set-Up Cost: It can cost a fortune to start a C corporation, depending on how the business is set up. Various costs apply in setting up a C corporation, including the fee that the corporation's shareholders pay. Service charges are evaluated when issuing the governing documents, outlining the structure of the company, entities in control, and background details of the company. This background details may include contact details, with the specific region, or state the company is situated.

There are several other public fines, as well as lawyers' service charges for filing the paperwork. They are also required to pay specific dues to the state for operations within their region.

High Taxation: Even though C corporations have relatively low tax rates for income of $75,000 or lower, this is usually not the norm if income grows above that. However, the lowest tax rate of a C corporation on income above $75,000 is 34 percent.

For most small businesses, a C corporation may be the best business structure. It would be best if you weighed the pros and cons of this business before making decisions on which is best for your small business.

It is said that less than 1% of tax lien properties end up in foreclosure. Therefore, if you are looking to buy a home, then this is definitely not the right path to follow. Numerous investors have been in this business for a while, and most of them have never experienced a foreclosure or known of a homeowner who was eventually unable to repay their back taxes.

Even then, if you do this long enough, you will probably end up with a property. Landing a property will mean a lot of things, such as hiring a lawyer to oversee the transfer, and so much more.

Chapter 7

Using Your Home for Business

---○---

This chapter will be walking you through some essential rules of home office deductions and allowable deductions when business owners use their homes for business. With the advent of advanced technology, running a small business has been made easier, such that most business owners only require their laptop computer, a phone, and an internet connection. They can work from wherever they want.

Many business owners still prefer working from a physical office rather than a virtual office. This is why most of them choose to use some part of their home for business.

This chapter aims to explain how the tax rules for home office deduction apply, especially the recently simplified home office deduction. Details of what beliefs a business owner may take or otherwise when using their home for business will also be discussed here. More so, the downsides concerning home office deductions, audit risks, and other issues that may emanate when such a home is put up for sale or sold will also be explained in this chapter.

The Simplified Home Office Deduction

The 43rd line of Form 8829 is used to claim Expenses for the Business Use of Your Home. This is also called the Home Office Deduction. The Internal Revenue Service, though seemingly slow, will always find ways to simplify the tax code by making them less complicated. For business owners who qualify for claiming a Home Office deduction, they need to understand the details of this new option:

- Deductions are limited to $1,500 per annum, based on $5 per sq. Ft.
- Depreciation deductions are disallowed.
- Schedule A of Form 1040 is used for mortgage interest and property tax deductions.
- All other actual expenses related to the home cannot be deducted.
- Loss cannot be carried forward.
- The simplified conventional method can be used for any taxable year.
- The business owner can choose a method using the timely filed original federal tax return technique for the taxable year.
- Any method chosen cannot be changed for the same year.
- Suppose the simplified method was used for Year 1 and the standard way for year 2. In that case, the depreciation deduction for Year 2 must be calculated using the appropriate optional depreciation table, whether the table was used in Year 1 or not, when the property was used for the business.

- With effect from 2018, the tax bill only allows for a deduction of up to $10,000 for the state, local, and property taxes on Schedule A and mortgage interest on new mortgages of up to $750,000 of debt. If the business owner has amounts above these, the conventional method might be the best option. The Internal Revenue Service produces a table of summary for comparison of the two methods. They include:

- Both methods accept home office deductions for portions of the residence exclusively used for business regularly.

- The simplified method has an allowable space of only 300 sq. ft. In contrast, the conventional method considers the home percentage that was utilized for your business operation.

- The simplified method uses $5 per sq. Ft. in determining the home office deduction, while the conventional method considers the actual expenses incurred by the business and the records sustained.

- For the simplified method, all home-related deductions listed are fully claimed in Schedule A. In contrast, the Regular method apportions home-related listed premises to either Schedule A and Business Schedules C or F.

- The simplified method does not allow for business asset deductions that are depreciating. In contrast, the conventional method allows for the depreciation debit for the home's portion for the business.

- Suppose you sell your home; the simplified method does not recapture the depreciation accruing to this sale, while the conventional method allows for the reclaim of depreciation on income generated upon the sale of a home.

- For the simplified method, the deductions made cannot outstrip the aggregate income from the home's business use when subtracted from business expenses and the conventional way.

- For the simplified method, the amount atop the gross income limit may not be assigned to a later date, while for the conventional way, the excess atop the threshold may be transferred to a later date.

- For the simplified method, the loss carried over from using the previous year's conventional method may not be declared. Still, this same loss may be carried over for the traditional way if the traditional method was used during the last year and if the aggregate income test is attained in the current year.

Filling Out the Form 8829

Initially, the rule for the use of Form 8829 for home office deduction was made for taxpayers who use a portion of their home to perform administrative and management activities. This could be doctors who work in hospitals, salespersons who spend most of their time at customer's locations, tradespeople and artisans who spend their time at job sites but use a portion of their home to do their paperwork and follow up services. The sections below will explain who can use the Form, compare the simplified and regular methods, and explain the Form's different parts.

Who Uses the Form

The home office deduction can be claimed if there is a dedicated space in the home used to conduct business activities (for example, administrative or management). No other place or office is used to perform the same tasks. Please, it is worthy to note that the home office may not be where clients are met or where principal activities of the business are conducted. This means that performing an office duty at home does not qualify a taxpayer for this deduction. Neither does the space used for other personal activities example, utilizing the dining table to eat and after that work, because freedom is not solely dedicated as a workspace. Suppose the dining room has a space set aside exclusively for work-related activity with equipment like a desk, computer, and probably a printer. In that case, such a person is entitled to ask for a home office deduction.

Furthermore, if a portion of the home is used to store samples or inventory, this entitles you to a home office deduction claim example, cosmetics.

Business owners can use Form 8829 either as a renter and a homeowner.

- ✓ For a homeowner, the total cost of maintaining the home must be computed, and this has to include mortgage interests, taxes, depreciation, repairs, and insurance. Also, all cleaning services for the entire home are calculated, and then the percentage you use for business is deducted.

✓ For a renter, accurately calculate the total rent, including utilities, insurance, and cleaning, and then deduct the portion used for business.

Determining Your Home Office Space

Form 8829, complete lines 1 through 7 to determine the portion of the home that is used exclusively for business:

✓ On line 1, enter the area in square feet of the home apportioned for business use.

✓ On line 2, enter the total area of the home.

✓ On line 3, divide line 1 by line 2 to determine the percentage of the home used for business and enter the result as a percentage because that is the percentage of the expenses for the home concerning interest, depreciation, utility costs, real estate taxes, and repairs which will determine the deduction.

✓ On line 7, enter your deduction percentage from line 3 and skip lines 4 to 6. But if the home is used as a day-care center, then lines 4 to 6 will be used to calculate the percentage of the house used as a day-care center, then multiply the result from line 6 by the number on line 3 and enter the product online 7.

Calculating Your Home Office Deduction

In calculating the home office deduction, specific considerations detailed below must be noted:

- On line 8, enter the amount from line 29 of your Schedule C, which is the net earnings after expenses, plus any net gain or loss is shown on Schedule D of Form 1040 or Form 4797 (Sales of Business Property). Note that the home office deduction cannot exceed this amount.

- On lines 9 through 22, the column deals with expenses that apply exclusively to your office example: repairs and maintenance.

- On lines 9 through 22, column b is for expenses that apply to the entire house, which the Internal Revenue Service refers to as indirect costs. It is worthy to note that if the house is on a lease, the rent paid is recorded on column b of line 18.

- On lines 23 through 35, this deals with many calculations and figures based on all previous models inputted.

- On line 36, allowable deductions are inputted here and carry the same over to line 30 on schedule C.

It is worthy to note that one can deduct real estate taxes, insurance, mortgage interest, depreciation, utilities, and repairs related to the business area in having a home office. The balance of these is deducted on Schedule A subject to official tax limits. For a lease, rent expenses accrued from the business portion are also removed.

Also, it is worthy to note that if one had more home office expenses in the past year than one could use, the remaining amount from the previous year's Form 8829 should be added on line 25 of the current year's Form 8829. This also goes for excess losses from the past year's Form 8829 added to the current year's line 31.

Calculating the Home Office Depreciation Allowance

For homeowners who are business owners, the home office depreciation percentage on line 7 of Form 8829 is applied to the home's depreciation allowance on a line-by-line breakdown of the Form's right part.

The Value of the Home

This is dealt with on line 37, where depreciation deduction is computed. When the home office is set up, the percentage claimed as office space in the home is written off. It is worthy to note that residential property is usually written off over 27 ½ years. Still, once it is included for business and considered business property, it has a longer life. On this same line, the smaller payment for the home and the original, renovation/remodeling, and closing costs or market value as at when it involved the business is entered. This only applies from when a home office deduction claim was initiated.

Exclusion of Land

On line 38, the home's land's value is deducted from the home's cost to know the home's net worth. This is so because; property cannot be depreciated in this regard. In most cases, 15% is allocated for the land unless the exact amount can be determined, and in some cases, the percentage is higher for some high-brow regions.

Basis of the Building

On line 39, the home basis is calculated by subtracting line 38 from 37.

Business Area of the Home

On line 40, multiply line 39 by home office deduction percentage from line 7. This is the percentage of the area of the home used for business that can be written off.

Percentage Depreciation

On line 41, the depreciation percentage is calculated, which depends mainly on when the home office was set up. If it was set up before 12 May 1993, it is a 31 ½-year write-off, and post 12 May 1993 is over 39 years write-off. If the home office was after 12 May 1993, but before 2012, the percentage is 2.564%, except in the following exceptions:

- The home office came after 12 May 1993 and before 1994, but construction started, or there was a binding contract to buy or build the home before 13 May 1993.
- The home office came after 12 May 1993, and the home stopped being used for business before the end of the year.
- The home office came after 1986 and before 13 May 1993.
- The home office came before 1987.

For these exceptions, please refer to Publication 946 for further guidance and bear in mind that you don't take the full percentage in the first year the home office is set up.

Allowable Depreciation

To determine the depreciation deduction based on the use of the home for business by multiplying line 40 by 41. This amount is then entered on lines 42 and 30 of Form 8829.

It is worthy to note that many people shy away from depreciating their homes because some do not understand how depreciation works. Others may find it difficult trying to figure out their home's adjusted basis. Others think that if they depreciate, they may have difficulties calculating profit or loss on their house's sale later. The Internal Revenue Service states that a home's value has depreciated, whether deducted or noted. When the home is to be sold, the depreciation may be required to be recaptured, even when the deduction was not taken as part of home office deductions on tax returns.

Carryover of Leftovers

Please note that loss cannot be taken because of home office deduction, but excess determination can be carried over to another year's tax return. On lines 43 and 44, the home office deduction that couldn't be deducted is computed. This can be removed in the future, provided that enough income is available.

Recall that on Schedule A, the 80% balance of total mortgage interest from line 10b of Form 8829 and the balance of total real estate taxes from line 11b are deducted. Line 8 of Schedule A captures mortgage interest balance, while line 5 of Schedule A captures real estate taxes. For instance, if business income is $12,000, business expenses are $10,000, and home office expenses are $3,000, of which $2,000 is apportioned to mortgage interest and real estate tax for the use of the office.

Deduct the interest and taxes of $2 000, which leaves a balance of $10 000 for possible deductions. Deduct $10 000 for business expenses, and this will bring income to zero; Carryover the remaining $1,000 to the next year. If there is no sufficient income to deduct from next year, carry it over again to the subsequent year.

Chapter 8

Deducting Your Entertainment Expenses

You can deduct your expenses by following a set of rules while doing what you love to do. Most entertainment expense deductions are limited to 50 percent, but there are exceptions to that rule. For example, suppose you went to dinner with a business prospect and a business reason for the meal or entertainment you are participating in. In that case, you can deduct it from your taxes as a business expense. There must be a business purpose for the meal or entertainment; it has to take place where you can conduct business, and if you run a business before, during, or after, you can legally deduct the meal.

The important part about being able to deduct your entertainment or meal is to audit-proof these activities. You can do this by keeping all of your receipts for business meals and entertainment, especially those that are over $75. Write down who was at your business meeting, their occupations, official titles, and any other information needed to show a business relationship. Also include the time, date, and location of where the entertainment took place, write down a specific reason why the business meeting took place, and list how much it cost (being sure to keep your receipt if it's over $75.) If you keep these records in a timely fashion, you'll cover yourself if the IRS ever audits you.

Now let's say that you want to entertain a business client outside of a business setting. In this case, you're allowed to deduct 50 percent of your entertainment expense if it's "associated entertainment." Associated entertainment takes place in a non-business setting where there is no business discussion. As long as you have a business discussion on the same day preceding or following the associated entertainment, then you can deduct this cost from your taxes. Again, be sure to keep track of who you met with, where it occurred, why it occurred, and the amounts of money you spent to audit-proof your return.

Suppose you would like your significant other to join you during an entertainment event. In that case, you can as long as the person you are discussing business with also brings their significant other along. You can't deduct a meal with just yourself and your spouse or significant other because the IRS knows that you are closely connected, but as long as you tie it into the business meeting and your business associate brings someone else along, you can deduct the expense.

To track your cost of personal meals, you can list down how much you usually spend on food and expense the excess cost of your food over your average meal price. This also works the same way if you split the cost of a business meal with your business partner, known as a Dutch-treat deduction.

There are a few exceptions where you can deduct the full cost of your expenses instead of just 50%. If you are engaging in an activity that is a business promotion, you can deduct your expenses' full cost. Home entertainment can also be removed, sometimes more so than going out to eat at a restaurant. As long as you conduct business with the people you are entertaining, as long as it doesn't seem like a personal event, then you can deduct the cost of your food and beverages 100%.

Deducting Your Vacation Costs

While you're on a business trip, you can deduct 100 percent of the on-the-road expenses, such as the cost of lodging, laundry, and dry cleaning. You can remove half of your food expenses while traveling as well. The only thing you need to do is stay somewhere other than your home or a place where you often go. As long as you spend the night in an area that you rarely go to, the trip is considered business travel.

You can also deduct the costs of your spouse or significant other by employing them in your business. He or she has to have a reason for accompanying you on the trip, and if your partner can earn you income while on the trip or has licensed in the business, you can deduct their expenses as well.

If your business trip takes you to a foreign destination, you can also claim that the weekends are business days if you conduct business on the Friday and Monday of the trip. Even if you aren't working, your expenses are tax-deductible. This also works on Federal holidays, allowing you to vacation and save money on taxes every year. Even the days you travel to your destination are considered business days as long as you take a direct route and don't have too many non-business diversions.

When you take your business vehicle to go on a trip, you're still able to deduct the traveling cost. Up to 300 miles per day can be deducted from your taxes, so split up travel days to make use of this. All of the lodging and meal expenses can be removed, except for the cost of taking additional people, so if you were to spend $50 for a single room and it costs $75 to get a double room, you can deduct the $50 and the leftover $25 is a nondeductible expense.

Cruises can also be tax-deductible if you attend the right ones. If you follow a cruise that is hosting a convention related to your business and more than half of the time you're on the cruise, you are spending time on business; you can deduce up to $2,000 a year. The cruise has to be registered as a U.S. vessel, and the port has to be in the U.S., but as long as you take the log of the business activity you do each day and the number of hours you spent in business seminars. Conventions and conferences are also tax deductible if you spend at least half of your regular working hours conducting business activities, even if it doesn't happen to be on a cruise.

Making Sure That You Are Audit-Proof

To gain the maximum amount of deductions for your home-based business, you have to keep good documentation of your activities. Expenses under $75 usually don't have to be proven with receipts except for when it comes to lodging receipts. You must keep good records of where you went and what you did and keep receipts from your on-the-road travel separate from your transportation expenses.

Keep a log, diary, or tax organizer to list down all of your expenses on the day that it happens to prove to the IRS what money you spent. When you go to conventions and seminars, you should explain the number of days you spent there and confirm that you had more business days than personal days. When you travel outside of the U.S., more than two-thirds of the days you travel should be business days. If you can maintain good records, then these expenses are 100% tax-deductible. To prove that a trip is for business, you can also document business intent for the journey by listing correspondence sent to business partners, emails, and phone calls.

Keeping useful information is also essential when it comes to transportation expenses. As a home-based business owner, you can deduct the mileage when you drive for business use. The percentage of time you use your vehicle for personal and business use determines how deductible your business automobile is. If you don't keep good records about your driving, your transportation costs won't be tax-deductible.

To keep good records, you should list the total miles, the whole business miles, the unlimited commuting miles, and other personal miles whenever you drive. The documents should show that you are using your vehicle for business use, and although you don't need to write down all the traveling, you do daily. You can get away with listing your miles at the end of the week, and it's easiest to write down the information whenever you get in your car to drive home.

There are a few options that you have when it comes to logging your miles for the IRS. You can create a one-day log where you list all the times you use your car, the nature of your trip and determine the amounts of mileage for each stop. This is quite a bit of information, so you can create a 90-day log if that's too tedious. You follow the same process for 90 days to substantiate how you use your vehicle the rest of the year if you follow similar driving patterns for the whole year.

The third option that you have is to log your miles is to use the first-week rule. During this time, you keep an automobile log for the first week of each month and show that your business use was similar during the rest of the month. You still list out your appointments, but you only have to calculate the mileage you use for the first week of every month. The fourth option is to list only your personal use for 90 days and compare the odometer to find the percentage of time you spend using your vehicle for business and personal reasons. This option is a lot easier for most people, and it's easy to figure out how many miles you use your car for business transportation with some simple math.

The Different Financial Statements

As we have mentioned a few times in this guidebook, some financial documents are essential to your business. These documents will help you keep your finances in line, help you know whether you are making accurate entries into the ledger, and can even assist you when you need to bring in investors or lenders to grow your business.

As an owner of a small business, you need to have a good understanding of some of these basic statements to get a good look at where the company stands financially. This is where it is essential for you to always communicate with the bookkeeping.

There are quite a few different financial statements that you could look at. The one that you want to work with will depend on what you are interested in finding out. But the most common ones, and the ones that are often seen as the most important, include:

- The cash flow statement
- The owner's equity statement
- The income statement
- The balance sheet

These are considered the big four because they will give you a good picture of where your business is standing financially. They are also the statements that you need to show your investors to make decisions about whether they will work with you or not. Let's look at each one and see how they work and why they are crucial for your business.

You must make sure that you fill out these financial statements regularly. Most companies will do one each quarter of their business, and then they do this at the end of the year. There are several benefits to doing this. First, it is required for all publicly traded companies through the SEC. You need to submit these four documents to the SEC at these times to remain on the stock exchange.

You will find that many of your investors and lenders will take a look at these financial statements. They can get a good view of your financial state and make smart decisions about whether they want to invest in you or give you a loan. Without this information, the investors and the lenders won't even consider you. So, even if the SEC didn't require that you submit this information to them, it can still be useful if you need a business loan to fund something, like new equipment or an expansion, or to help convince investors that your business is a good option.

Another benefit of using these financial statements is that they give you a good view of your business's financial information. You will be able to fill them out pretty quickly if you have been keeping good records through the other tips that we talked about. You can then compare this information with the financial statements you completed in previous quarters and years to let you know your financial state's trends and make the right decisions to prepare you for the future.

The Balance Sheet

The first financial document we will look at is the balance sheet. This one is going to use the formula assets = liabilities + equity. Within this particular statement, you will see that these three areas are divided to show which of your business accounts are listed under the owner's equity, liabilities, and assets.

The owner's equity will represent the earnings that are retained for your business. You will see that all of the accounts on this balance sheet do not have to keep a $0 balance. Generally, the stores with a $0 ratio are not on the balance sheet.

You can pick from two types of formats for your balance sheet. You can choose from either the horizontal or the vertical structures. Most businesses prefer to work with a vertical design. But if you want to work more with the accounting equation before, you will want to work with the horizontal format.

Based on your business's assets, the company will be balanced in all the obligations of a business financially. This will include investments and any retained earnings. Think about it this way. Assets are the means a company uses to operate. Owner's equity and liabilities are the two main ways that you can support these assets.

The balance sheet will be the financial statement that will report all of the assets and liabilities of the company and the shareholders' equity, basing this on a specific point in time. It will provide you with a basis for computing rates of return and then evaluate the business's capital structure.

The neat thing about the balance sheet is that it is perfect for providing a snapshot of the company, what that company owes and owns, and some information about the amount that shareholders have invested. It can go in-depth or just give an overview of the finances of the business.

Many investors and lenders will take a look at the balance sheet. They need to look at some of the other financial statements to get the best view of how they are economical. But the balance sheet is the right place for the lenders and the investors to see a summary or a snapshot of the company before going further.

Interpreting the balance sheet is not meant to be complicated. This statement is a snapshot that represents the state of the company finan- cially in just one moment. By itself, it is not going to show you the trends of the company that have played out over time. Because of this reason, when you are attempting to interpret the balance sheet, you need to compare it with some previous balance sheets. So if you are looking at the balance sheet for the fourth quarter of the company, you should compare it to the balance sheets for the third, second, and first quarters to see the numbers and the trends over the past year.

Also, it is a good idea to take those balance sheets and then compare them to other businesses that are considered to work in the same industry. This gives you a good idea of whether the company is doing well compared to the industry trends. Please don't reach a company's balance sheet to those in different industries because each industry will have its financing approaches, confusing.

Now that you know a bit more about the balance sheet, it is essential to understand what accounts need to be listed in each section. These are the owner's equity, liability, and assets. Let's divide each part up to see what will be inside each one on the balance sheet.

Current Assets

The items that you put inside the current assets are the ones that will have a lifespan of a year or less. The business then plans to convert those assets into cash. Some of the items that you can put into the part of the current assets of the balance statement include:

- Short-term obligations that you owe to the clients
- Accounts receivable
- U.S. Treasuries
- Cash

- Cash and cash equivalents
- Raw materials
- Inventory

Non-Current Assets

These assets are the ones that can't be turned into cash as quickly. These are the ones that are expected to be turned into cash within a year, or they could have a longer life span of more than a year. These are the ones that will usually have depreciation associated with them as well. Some examples of these types of assets include:

- Copyright
- Patents
- Goodwill
- Intangible assets
- Land
- Buildings
- Computers
- Machinery
- Tangible assets

Liabilities

When you are looking at your liabilities, you will consider this as the obligations that the business owes to others. Just like assets, these can include both long-term and current liabilities. Some of the penalties that will be found in this column of the balance statement include:

- Non-debts that are more than one year old

- Debts that are more than one year
- Long-term liabilities
- Accounts payable
- Paid within a year
- Current liabilities

Owner's Equity

This is the money that the owner has invested inside of their business. The retained earnings shown on your income statement will be transferred into the owner's equity at the end of your fiscal year. The owner's equity is going to show the net worth of the business. You will have a capital account or a drawing account. The capital account is going to be any money invested or earned by the company. The drawing version is going to be the money that is withdrawn from the company.

The Income Statement

When you first take a look at the business statement, there is a lot of information, which can seem scary. However, once you know what is inside it, you will find that this statement can be beneficial. The income statement will take a closer look at all the sales and all the expenses of that business. The business can usually choose to do this quarterly and annually through their fiscal year to keep track of things.

An income statement is another financial statement that will be responsible for reporting a company's financial performance over a specific period of accounting. The financial performance will be assessed by providing a summary to lenders and investors about how the business will incur all its revenues and expenses through both its non-operating and operating activities.

The income statement is often going to be known as the profit and loss statement, and it is one of the three financial statements that need to be present in the annual report of the company and the 10-K. All public companies will need to submit these documents legally to the SEC and the investor public. The other two sheets that are submitted simultaneously will be the cash flows statement and the balance sheet.

These three are essential because they can provide the investors and the lenders with a lot of information about a business's state of finances. Still, the income statement is unique because it is the only one that will summarize the sales and the net income of the company.

Unlike what you would do with the company balance sheet, the income statement will provide the performance information about a specific time. While the balance sheet will say how the business is when the business owner filled out the sheet, the income statement will provide information over a year, a quarter, or a year based on how the company records this information. The income statement will start with the company's sales and then work its way down to the net income and then the earnings per share.

Two main parts need to be present on the income statement, no matter what type of company you are running. These two parts are the non-operating and the operating. With the operating portion of this financial statement, you will disclose all the information about any revenues and expenses that the company incurred directly from regular business operations. For example, if you are a business that sells sports equipment, you would make your money by selling these pieces of equipment. This information would be recorded in the operating section of this statement. The income statement also needs to include the non-operating area. This will disclose all the information about expenses and revenue for any activities that aren't a part of the company's regular operations. If your company sells investment securities or real estate in addition to your everyday work, then you would list any profits you made from those sales in the non-operating section. You may hear many different terms when it comes to the income statement. You may listen to about income, earnings, and profits. These all mean the same thing, so keep this in mind when you hear them. There are also two raw formats that you can use with the income statement, the single-step format or the multi-step format.

The Multi-Step Format

Some of the parts that are going to be shown in the multi-step format include:

- Net sales
- Cost of sales
- Gross income
- Selling, general, and administrative expenses
- Taxes
- Pretax income
- Other income and expenses
- Operating income

- Net income after taxes

The Single-Step Format

Some of the steps that come with the single-step format include:

- Net income
- Taxes
- Pretax income
- Other income and expenses
- Research and development expenses
- Marketing and administrative
- Materials and production
- Net sales

You can choose the method that works the best for your business and includes all the information about your finances.

Statement of Owner's Equity

The next financial statement to look at is the Owner's Equity Statement. This is a financial document that can be used either on its own as a separate statement, or it can be something included in the income statements or the balance sheet. It is sometimes also known as a Statement of Retained Earnings. This is the statement that will let you show the standing of your business earnings.

Often you will see this type of statement in a corporation that has a lot of shareholders and pays out dividends. But you can still find it useful with your small business to show your financial standings and your retained earnings. The main reason to use this statement is to release all this financial information to the public, giving the public the information they need to decide if they would like to invest in the business. It is also an excellent tool to analyze how healthy your business is.

The statement of owner's equity will represent the value of a business after meeting all of its obligations through a specific period. This statement is responsible for showing the movement of capital throughout that company. It will reflect the amount that the owner or owners invested into the company and any profits that the business has been able to generate that is then reinvested directly into the company. The reinvested income will be known as retained earnings on this sheet.

This statement will report the changes in the owner's equity over some time, and this period is usually going to be for each year. As a small business, there is a chance that you won't need to use this statement because smaller firms are more likely to report the retained earnings on the balance sheet instead.

If you decide that your business needs to prepare the statement of owner's equity, you will want to prepare it after you are done with the income statement. This is because this particular statement will need to have the net income or the net loss for the period. But you can prepare this before the balance sheet because the owner's equity will need to be on the balance sheet.

This statement is a good one to use because it will help you see a business's financial health. It can also give you some insight into whether or not the company has sufficient cash flow to help fund its operations without needing the aid of any outside investment.

Most of the time, you don't want to see a company reinvest their profits into the business because this can show that they are not doing a great job handling their cash flow. If the industry is increasing, the owners may decide to invest some capital to help fund additional wages, accounts receivable, and inventory to help them keep up. This is acceptable because that money will quickly be made back shortly once they catch up a bit.

The problem is if the business is not able to support itself financially without these capital infusions. If the business makes this statement and cannot help itself without these infusions of capital, then the creditors are not likely to work with the company, and it can be hard to get the loan that you need to run your business.

Chapter 9

Common Tax Deductions for Small Businesses

As a small business, you can claim several expenses as legitimate deductions to your taxable income, so you will pay the lowest possible income taxes. What are these expenses? Here's a list of a few of the most common ones.

Business-Related Food Expenses

For qualified food and drink purchases related to your small business's conduct, you can deduct as much as 50% of the total amount. What makes such purchases qualified?

The first requirement is that obviously, it was related to the business. Family meals and treating friends out to lunch do not count. But if it is used to meet with and treat a potential client to coffee or dinner, it is considered business-related. The second requirement is that such purchases need to be properly supported by documents like official receipts or invoices. These pieces of information must be on the supporting papers:

- Location off the meal
- date when the meal took place
- How are you or your business's representative related to the people or person the meal was shared with
- The meal's total cost

The most practical and accurate way to be on top of your business's meal expenses is by keeping official receipts and writing notes at the back.

Business Travel Expenses

You can deduct 100% of all qualified business-related travel expenses when you file your business's income tax returns. These include plane tickets, hotel check-ins, meals, and car rental expenses, among others.

How to make sure these are really qualified? The most important characteristics include:

- The trip is absolutely needed for your business
- You must travel outside of your tax-registered business address, i.e., outside the city or state where your small business conducts its normal operations
- The trip must last longer than one normal business day
- The travel requires sleeping or resting on the route

Business Related Vehicle Use

If the vehicle is used solely for the business, you may deduct 100% of all related expenses. But if it is used for both business and personal activities, you may only claim the business-related portion of the expenses.

You can do this in two ways: using actual mileage for the period or using The IRS prescribed standard mileage rates per mile driven. As the name of the first option implies, you will compute the percentage of business-related mileage to the total distance for the period and multiply it by the period's vehicle use related total expenses. If you choose to use the IRS' standard mileage rates, just multiply it by the period's total mileage.

Insurance Premiums

Whatever you pay to ensure your business's assets, you can use as a legitimate tax deduction come filing time. But if you are holding office at home or use part of it to run your business, you can use your renter's insurance costs as taxable income deductions.

Expenses Related to Running a Home Office

Based on the simplified home office expense guidelines issued by the IRS, you can deduct $5 per square foot of the area of your home dedicated to running a small business or doing freelancing work up to a maximum area of 300 square feet. To qualify for this deduction, two conditions must be satisfied. First, the area must be for the exclusive use of the business only. Here, you cannot clean deductions if you run your small business from your dining room because it is not exclusively used for the business. The dining room will still be there even if you didn't run your business from home. Second, the whole office area must be used regularly as the primary place of your business's operations. It must be your headquarters.

Supplies

For as long as you use office supplies for your small business in the year in which you bought them, you can claim their purchase costs as tax deductions. These include:

- Paper
- Pens
- Printer cartridges
- Paper clips
- Other work-related consumable items

Always remember to keep the official receipts to make sure proper documentation and support for filing them as tax deductions.

Communications Expenses

If your small business is heavily reliant on using the phone and the Internet, then you can claim expenses related to these as tax deductions, but if you use them for both personal and business activities, you can only claim a certain percentage of the expenses attributable to your small business as tax deductions.

Let's say your monthly Internet bills average around $50. If you use it for business three-fourths of the time, then you can claim 75% of that monthly expense - or 37.5 dollars - as tax deductions.

Bank Fees and Interest on Loans

If you fund part of your operations using bank financing, you can use the interest paid on borrowed money as tax deductions. If you have business-related credit cards, interest and charges on these qualify as tax deductions too. Again, the qualifier here is that they are directly related to your small business's operations.

Depreciation Expenses

These pertain to the annual writing off of the cost of big-ticket capital items like vehicles, equipment, and improvements done on the office's premises. Instead of deducting the entire cost as a onetime expense, assets like these are capitalized in your business's books of accounts. The entire cost is amortized over the next several years as depreciation expense.

The amount of depreciation expense claimed annually depends on the chosen method. The most common one is the straight-line method, which divides the total asset cost over its estimated useful life as expressed in several years.

For example, you spent $10,000 on improving a condominium unit used as your small business's primary office. Your estimated useful life for the improvements is ten straight-line depreciation expense using the straight-line method is $1000. This is the amount of depreciation on the asset you can claim as deductions when you file your business's annual income tax.

Service or Professional Fees

When your small business needs to hire professionals to help in its operations, you can use the money you pay them as tax deductions.

These include the retainer fees of your accountant, lawyer, or bookkeeper, among others. You may also include tax-deductible service or professional fees or the cost of subscribing to an accounting or bookkeeping software such as QuickBooks.

If you need more information regarding tax-deductible professional or service fees, check out the IRS' guidelines for legal and professional fees.

Employee Salaries and Benefits

If your small business has employees, you may also claim their salaries, paid leaves, and other benefits as tax deductions if you meet several requirements. These include:

- The employee is not an owner, partner, or member of the business
- The salary paid is both necessary and reasonable
- The employee was able to do his or her duties and responsibilities to the business

Donations to Charitable Institutions

If you have a philanthropic heart, your business may also benefit from helping qualified organizations. Your business may use qualified donations as tax deductions depending on its structure. If yours is a single proprietorship, partnership, or a limited liability corporation (LLC), you may claim the deductions on your personal tax returns. But if it's a corporation, you may claim the charitable donations on your business's corporate tax filings.

Learning Costs

You may use educational expenses meant for the business's economic benefit as legitimate deductions for your small business. What do these educational expenses look like? If you are running a printing business and you enroll in a seminar that helps you learn how to use a cutting-edge graphic design software like Photoshop, you can use the fee as a tax deduction for your small business.

If you're operating a small coffee shop and you enroll in an Udemy course on how to brew the perfect coffee, you can claim the cost of the e-course when you file your or your business's tax returns.

These must help you become better at what you do for your business or maintain your expertise or qualifications. That way, the enterprise can grow. The following are education-related expenses that qualify as tax deductions for your small business:

- Courses and classes directly relevant to your business or line of work
- Webinars and seminars
- Subscriptions to publications related to your business or profession
- Books or e-books related to your industry

Dependent and Child Care

While these may look like personal expenses on the surface, you may claim them as tax-deductible expenses for your small business. For example, care-related costs for your children 12 years old or younger are eligible as tax-deductible expenses. If adult dependents require professional care because of mental or physical disabilities, such as your spouse or parents, you may also claim their professional care expenses. Ask for the deductions when you file your personal or business income tax returns.

Energy Efficiency-Related Costs

Believe it or not, The IRS gives credit to taxpayers who do their best to improve their home or office is energy efficiency. Expenses incurred for making the home or business premises more energy efficient entitle you or your small business a 30% tax credit or deduction. This means if you spent $1000 to install energy efficiency devices such as solar panels, wind turbines, or solar water heaters, you could claim a $300 tax deduction on this expense. For more details on this, the IRS provides details on home energy tax credits on their website.

Costs of Investments

Let us say you or your small business wants to take advantage of depressed stock prices to make extra income, and you borrow money to do so. You can claim the interest paid on loan as tax deductions, but you can only do so up to the amount of interest that does not exceed the investment's income. If interest amounted to $100, but the income is only $50, you can only claim $50 in interest expenses as tax deductions for the borrowed money.

Medical Expenses

Whether it's medical care expenses (including your doctor's professional fees, medicines, or home care costs) or insurance premiums,

You can claim these expenses as deductions in your or your small business's tax returns. If you're self-employed and pay for your own Medicare, you can also claim dental and health care insurance premiums as deductions.

Property Taxes

When your small business pays real estate taxes at the local and state levels, you can claim them as valid tax deductions, but there is a maximum limit of $10,000 only.

Interest on Loans and Mortgages

If you borrowed money to finance the construction or improvement of your small business's office or your home, if you use it for running your enterprise, then you can claim interest payments as tax deductions. Even when you take out loans against your home or property equity, the interest on such a borrowed money can also be valid tax deductions.

Moving Expenses

If your business incurred moving expenses, then you may be able to use them as tax deductions, but it must first pass a distance test. The distance of your new business location from the old one must be at least 50 miles. Or if you move to a new home as part of your business operations, your new home must be at least the same distance away from your old one.

Retirement Account Contributions

If you are currently contributing to an IRA or an individual retirement account, you may use the number of your contributions as part of your tax deductions, especially if your small business is a sole proprietorship, partnership, or an LLC. This is because income earned from these types of businesses is taxed personally, i.e., you file their income taxes on your personal returns.

Marketing and Advertising Expenses

All expenses related to promoting and marketing your small business's products or services are tax deductible. These include website design, print and digital advertising, website maintenance, and business card printing.

Entertainment Expenses for Clients and Employees

As long as you discuss business with your clients during meetings, you may claim entertainment expenses of up to 50% of the actual amount. If you hold social events for your employees, you may even claim as much as 100% of the expenses as deductions.

Costs Related to Starting a Business

If you set up a new business on your latest tax year, you may claim up to $5000 in startup expenses related to it. These expenses include costs of training, travel, marketing, and other things necessary for setting up the new enterprise.

Conclusion

Understanding taxes doesn't have to be complicated. If you want to build wealth and secure your family's financial future, you must understand how tax laws work and how to pay as little as legally possible toward taxes. With the simple tricks that you have learned about the benefits of starting a home-based business, you'll be able to save lots of money on the things that you already do and at the places that you already go. It also allows you to travel, speak to people, and share what you love to do with the world.

The most important thing is that you take action and start your home-based business. Prepare yourself for the changes that you have to make to meet the IRS requirements. Start taking the right notes about your daily activities, learn how to log your mileage, and start saving receipts whenever you go out to eat with business partners. It might seem like a hassle at first, but the significant saving that you receive from building a home-based business will pay off for years to come.

Now that you know some of the significant tax savings that you receive from starting a home-based business, now it's time to do it! You'll earn more income with a home-based business than you could with a second job, and you'll have the opportunity to travel around the world, meet new people, and sell your products and services to others. You can work primarily from home if you enjoy spending time alone, or you can use it as an opportunity to network with new people and live an exciting life. The tax laws benefit those who are self-employed and understand the many different tax benefits available for business owners.

Discussion section

Setting up your business is a fantastic process, one that includes managing a variety of details. You must handle the production of your goods or services, delivery of goods or services, marketing, managing employees, addressing the needs of your customers, tracking income and expenses, and creating the processes and procedures that will help your business run.

Part of the process of setting up your business is finding a way to manage all your financial information effectively without it dominating your administration tasks, and that means choosing the right accounting service software to complement your business needs. While there are various services and software available, it is essential to choose one that can grow with your business, allowing you to upgrade as needed.

QuickBooks is an accounting service software that allows you to automate bookkeeping tasks which are the basis of all the financial information for your business. It can provide various options and versions, making it possible to find what you need for your business with ease. Plus, as your business grows, there are upgrade options that allow you to add what you need when you need it.

It is important to note that many of the options available through QuickBooks can be accessed through its mobile applications, giving you the ability to categorize or input transactions when you are on the go. For self-employed individuals, these mobile functions can be a way to minimize how much time you spend inputting transactions at the end of a business trip or position since you can do it at the moment.

Other applications through QuickBooks are customized to be useful for small to medium-sized businesses, giving you the ability to match your business to the right software version. There are other benefits to using QuickBooks accounting service software, particularly related to accessing capital for expanding your business and funding capital investments.

Use QuickBooks to Apply for Financing

Even applying for additional financing can be done through Quick-Books Capital, using the financial data you already have available in your QuickBooks, making the application process fast and easy. So, what is QuickBooks Capital?

It is a service offered by Intuit Financing, Inc., which provides business loans to eligible QuickBooks clients. Using a holistic viewpoint, QuickBooks Capital looks to create funding options that are right for your business. There are two different funding options available:

- Directly underwriting loans

- Providing a marketplace to explore and be matched with curated lenders

For those individuals who use QuickBooks Online, you can apply for and receive short-term working capital loans. Factors that can impact your funding qualification include past business history, your use of QuickBooks Online, personal and business credit history, and your current liabilities.

Generally, QuickBooks Capital requires a FICO score of 580, no personal or business bankruptcies in the past two years, and at least $50,000 in revenue over the past year. There are also businesses on the prohibited business list, so you need to make sure your business is not on that list before applying. Each application is viewed individually, so there is some discretion, and not everyone who meets the necessary application criteria will receive a loan.

The Capital Marketplace allows you to shop loan terms, lines of credit, and more. You can see your options without impacting your credit score and select the right funding option for your needs. At that point, you will have to complete the lending process with your financing partner chosen.

Even if you are going through a more traditional financing option, your QuickBooks financial statements can be used as part of your application process. There are a variety of uses and benefits to using Quick-Books as your accounting service software.

Determining What Is Right For Your Business

Throughout this guide, the focus has been on introducing you to all the options and versions offered by QuickBooks. It gives you the ability to customize your accounting software to meet your business's needs now and in the future as you continue to grow. Along the way, you have learned about the various offerings, which are targeted for businesses that are just starting, self-employed individuals, and even medium-sized companies with several employees.

What makes QuickBooks appealing is that you can access services through its online platform, allowing you to know that your data is continually being backed up, which means you don't have to worry about it being lost if your hardware should fail or your server were to go down for any unexpected reason. For small businesses, having the means to back up their financial data is key to allowing their business to survive and thrive even after a disaster, such as a tornado, flood, or fire.

Your business plan should include a disaster plan and the means to access your data, possibly from another location. With QuickBooks software being available in five online versions, you can have the peace of mind that comes from knowing your data is not lost just because your building or business location suffered damage.

However, QuickBooks also offers options for those who prefer to keep their software in-house, with desktop versions. It should also be noted that these versions can allow you to give access to your business accountant, making it easy for you to transfer financial information each quarter and during tax season.

To determine the best option for your business, ask yourself these critical questions:

- Am I self-employed, a sole proprietor, a limited liability company (LLC), or a Corporation?
- Will I have employees? If so, how many?
- Do I want to use timekeeping software, or do I prefer a handwritten timekeeping method for my employees?
- Are my employees going to be mobile, or will they be located primarily in our main office or production facility?
- Will I be doing my bookkeeping in-house, or is it being completed by an accountant?
- What is my budget for accounting software?
- Do I need regular updates and regular access to support for my software?
- Would I prefer a one-time cost or a subscription with a monthly or annual fee?
- Will I need financing or working capital?
- Do I have a business plan?
- What is my projected growth? Am I looking to expand my business into new markets?

All these questions can help you to determine the type of QuickBooks software you need and whether an online or desktop version will work for you. As part of your decision-making process, it is essential to weigh the costs involved. While the Self-Employed Online Version's monthly subscription cost is under $20, other versions of QuickBooks can come at a much greater cost.

For instance, using the payroll option could incur costs per employee, a base cost for the service, and additional costs for direct deposit or filing of tax forms and payments. While these costs might seem small at first, they could become more of a budget buster as your business grows. Therefore, it is essential to keep in mind that you can move up to a version that offers more options as part of the base subscription price to offset some costs.

It is important to note that you can contact QuickBooks to customize your experience and allow their trained staff to help you find the right options for your needs. They are going to focus on what your business needs now. Still, as your business grows, keep in mind that Quick-Books can grow with it.

Another aspect is that QuickBooks does a variety of calculations for you automatically. Individuals who use Excel spreadsheets find them-selves working harder to determine the right measures. As a business owner, time is money. Recognize that your time is valuable, and the more you must spend on your bookkeeping, the less time you have to get out there and make money by connecting with your customers and generating sales by meeting their needs.

For someone self-employed, your hourly rate maybe $40. If you spend three hours a week working on a spreadsheet, you have lost $120 of revenue. Using QuickBooks software can save you those three hours, allowing you to gain $120 in revenue for your business. Now that $20 a month for the subscription seems worth the cost. It is about under-standing the value of your time as a business owner and choosing the right tools to give you value-added benefits.

Granted, not every subscription will have the same monthly cost, but it is important to weigh those costs versus the benefits you receive from the software itself.

By opting for an accounting service software, you can cut the bookkeeping time down and give yourself more time to focus on growing your business and creating new opportunities to meet your customers' needs. This guide is meant to help you better understand what QuickBooks has to offer and how it can benefit your business. No matter if you are starting or are ready to move away from tracking expenses on a spreadsheet, QuickBooks can offer you the right fit. Exploring their options can be the first step in taking your business to a new and exciting level!

Frequently Asked Questions

Why is bookkeeping important for small businesses?

Bookkeeping is an essential and vital function that any small business must perform. This function will determine the long-term success of the company. Bookkeeping will help you develop the right idea about your business, and you can choose the future and growth of your business. It is easy to do this when you record every transaction. You can also understand the business's finances and make better plans and decisions for the future.

Accurate bookkeeping will also protect your business from any legal or financial assessments. For example, if you have trouble with a supplier or under audit by the IRS, you can get out of it if you have clean financial records. These records will also save you from paying any additional taxes. You can also uncover fraud and prevent it, whether it's from suppliers, employees, or vendors. Bookkeeping will also save you a lot of time to start right from managing invoices to payroll taxes; efficient bookkeeping will smooth out the various financial tasks you must perform. This will help you save a lot of time.

When should I ask for help?

If you are a small business owner, you can do everything by yourself. You should avoid spending money when you think you can take care of it, ask yourself. Most business owners use their capital to develop the product or service. Bookkeeping is one task that you should perform accurately. You should avoid making any bookkeeping errors since they can threaten your success and are very costly mistakes. For example, have you ever looked at a transaction and wondered where all the money came from? If you did ask yourself this question, you should get help with bookkeeping.

As a small business owner, you can use the following bookkeeping solutions to avoid making mistakes and reduce costs.

- Hire an in-house bookkeeper or accountant.
- Invest in accounting or bookkeeping software.
- Outsource the bookkeeping to an advisor or third-party company.

The first and third options are costly, but the individuals or companies will handle all the bookkeeping tasks. These methods will save you a lot of time and effort. If you want a cheaper solution, you can choose to purchase bookkeeping software. This will take care of all the basics, including reconciling bank transactions, generating financial statements, and adjusting account balances.

<-END->

I hope this book has been helpful for you to learn how to deduct taxes and build wealth. Go to savingssunrise.com for more more tips on saving money and creating wealth.

www.ingramcontent.com/pod-product-compliance
Lightning Source LLC
Chambersburg PA
CBHW070350220526
45467CB00001B/319